Peter Sherran

REVISION PLUS

Edexcel
GCSE Mathematics
Foundation

Revision and Classroom Companion

Contents

123	Number	Maths B – Units
4	Rounding Numbers	1, 2
5	Decimals	1, 2, 3
8	Number Properties	2
10	Whole Number Calculations	1, 2, 3
11	Integers	2, 3
13	Powers & Roots	2, 3
15	Order of Operations	1, 2, 3
16	Fractions	1, 2, 3
20	Percentages	1, 2, 3
23	Fractions, Decimals & Percentages	1, 2, 3
25	Everyday Maths	1, 3
27	Ratio & Proportion	1, 2
29	Estimating & Checking	1, 2

xy	Algebra	Maths B – Units
30	Algebraic Expressions	1, 2, 3
31	The Rules of Indices	2, 3
32	Substitution	2, 3
33	Brackets and Factorisation	2, 3
34	Linear Equations	3
36	Formulae	2, 3
38	Trial & Improvement	3
39	Sequences	2
41	Plotting Points	1, 2
42	Straight Line Graphs	1, 2
46	Linear Inequalities	3
47	Graphs of Quadratic Functions	3
49	Real Life Graphs	1, 2, 3

Contents

	Geometry	Maths B – Units
52	Angles	1, 2
54	Triangles	2, 3
56	Quadrilaterals	2, 3
57	Irregular Polygons	3
58	Regular Polygons	3
59	Symmetry	2
61	Congruence and Tessellation	2, 3
62	Similarity	2, 3
63	Pythagoras' Theorem	3
65	Perimeter	2
66	Area	2
68	Circles	2
70	Circles & Compound Area	3
71	Transformations	3
77	Constructions	3
80	Loci	3
81	3-D Shapes	2, 3
82	Nets & Elevations	2, 3
83	Volume	2, 3

	Measures	Maths B – Units
85	Maps and Scale Drawings	3
86	Enlargement, Area, Perimeter & Volume	3
87	Converting Measurements	1, 2
88	Bearings	3
89	Compound Measures	2
90	Measuring Lines & Angles	1, 2

	Probability	Maths B – Units
91	Probability	1

	Statistics	Maths B – Units
95	Problem Solving and Handling Data	1
96	Collecting Data	1
98	Sorting Data	1
101	Displaying Data	1
106	Averages and Spread	1
109	Formulae Sheet	
112	Index	

Rounding Numbers

Rounding a Number to 1 (or more) Decimal Places

If a number is given to 1 decimal place (1 d.p.), there is one digit after the decimal point. To round a number to 1 d.p., we must look at the **second** digit after the decimal point. There are two possibilities:

1. If the second digit after the decimal point is **4 or less** (i.e. 0, 1, 2, 3 or 4) we leave the first digit after the decimal point as it is.
2. If the second digit after the decimal point is **5 or more** (i.e. 5, 6, 7, 8 or 9) we **round up** by adding 1 to the first digit after the decimal point.

To round a number to 2 d.p. we must look at the **third** digit after the decimal point to decide whether we need to round up or to keep the second digit after the decimal point the same.

To round a number to 3 d.p. we must look at the **fourth** digit and so on. Unless a question tells you otherwise, always give money to 2 decimal places. Amounts of money are rounded to 2 d.p. in exactly the same way as below.

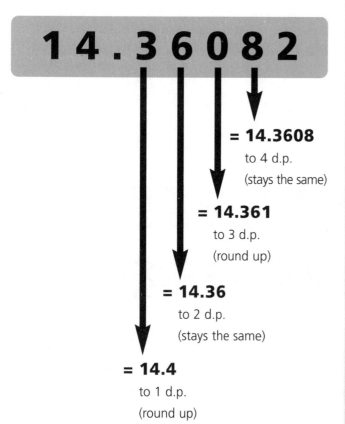

Rounding a Number to 1 (or more) Significant Figures

Rounding a number to a certain number of significant figures (s.f.) is very like rounding a number to a certain number of decimal places.

The number below shows the attendance at a pop concert. It has 4 significant figures.

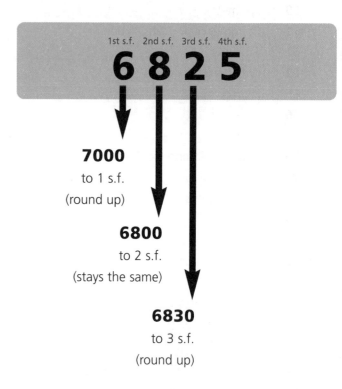

Notice how 0s are used to maintain the place value of the significant figures, e.g. 6825 is 7000 to 1 s.f. not 7.

Example

To round numbers less than 1 we follow the same rules except we start counting our significant figures from the first digit greater than 0 (zero).

1st s.f. 2nd s.f. 3rd s.f. 4th s.f.

0.03617

→ to 1 s.f. is **0.04** (round up)
→ to 2 s.f. is **0.036** (stays the same)
→ to 3 s.f. is **0.0362** (round up)

Decimals

Place Value in Decimal Numbers

All the digits in a whole number have a place value. In a decimal number, all digits to the right of the decimal point also have a place value.

Decimal Number	Place Value of Digits					
	10	1		$\frac{1}{10}$	$\frac{1}{100}$	$\frac{1}{1000}$
	Tens	Units	Decimal Point	Tenths	Hundredths	Thousandths
0.06		0		0	6	
0.507		0		5	0	7
1.39		1		3	9	
74.258	7	4		2	5	8

The position of the decimal point is just as important as the digits themselves. Misplacing the decimal point makes a huge difference because all the place values change. For example, in a long jump contest a pupil records a jump of 4.37m. Imagine the astonishment if the distance was recorded as 43.7m!

Decimals and Money

An amount of money is often written as a decimal, where the decimal point separates the amount in pounds from the amount in pence. Remember, any amount of money involving pounds and pence is always written to 2 decimal places (2 d.p.).

Examples

1. Six pounds forty seven pence is written as **£6.47**

2. Twelve pounds one pence is written as **£12.01 and not £12.1**

3. £5 can be written as **£5.00**

4. 47p can be written as **£0.47**

Recurring and Terminating Decimals

$\frac{1}{3}$ **as a decimal is 0.33333333...** and so on

$\frac{3}{11}$ **as a decimal is 0.27272727...** and so on

Both of these are examples of recurring decimals because one or more of the digits repeats itself continuously. To make a recurring decimal simpler we write the digit or digits that repeat continuously once and place a dot ($\cdot$) over them.

$\frac{1}{3}$ **= 0.33333333... = 0.$\dot{3}$**

$\frac{3}{11}$ **= 0.27272727... = 0.$\dot{2}\dot{7}$**

Decimals that do not recur are called terminating decimals. Fractions, written in their **simplest form**, will convert into terminating decimals **if** their denominators (bottom numbers) only have prime factors of **2** or **5** or **both**.

$\frac{7}{10}$ **= 0.7** (10 = 2 × 5)

$\frac{5}{8}$ **= 0.625** (8 = 2 × 2 × 2)

$\frac{19}{50}$ **= 0.38** (50 = 2 × 5 × 5)

Ordering Decimals

Ordering decimals means rearranging a series of decimals in either ascending (lowest to highest) or descending (highest to lowest) order. A useful method is to line up all the decimal points of the numbers in a vertical line. Then you can start with the first column on the left, and work along each column of numbers (left to right) to decide which is the highest number.

Example
Rearrange the following in ascending order:
0.54, 5.4, 0.45, 4.5

Line up the decimal points.

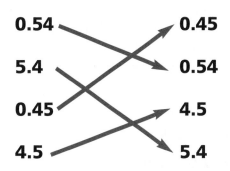

Decimals

Addition and Subtraction of Decimals

For addition and subtraction of decimals, the place values of the digits must line up one on top of the other, although an easy way is to line up your decimal points. Remember to bring the decimal point down to your answer.

Examples

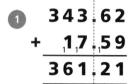

①
$$343.62$$
$$+ \ 17.59$$
$$\overline{361.21}$$

②
$$63.184$$
$$- \ 5.091$$
$$\overline{58.093}$$

Multiplication of Decimal Numbers by Powers of 10

To multiply a decimal number by a power of 10, e.g. 10 (10^1), 100 (10^2), 1000 (10^3), all you have to do is move all the digits a certain number of place values to the left. The number of place values moved is equal to the number of zeros (or the power). When you do this your number becomes bigger.

Examples

① $9.32 \times 10 = 93.2$

Digits move one place value to the left and the number becomes 10 times bigger.

② $0.047 \times 100 = 4.7$

Digits move two place values to the left and the number becomes 100 times bigger.

③ $13.27 \times 1000 = 13\ 270$

Digits move three place values to the left and the number becomes 1000 times bigger.

Multiplication of Positive Numbers by Decimal Numbers between 0 and 1

If you multiply any positive number by a decimal number between 0 and 1 the answer is always smaller than the positive number you started with.

Examples

① $10 \times 0.5 = 5$

② $5 \times 0.3 = 1.5$

③ $986 \times 0.01 = 9.86$

Multiplication of Decimal Numbers by Whole and Decimal Numbers

To multiply decimals, ignore the decimal points and multiply as you would whole numbers. You add the decimal point in at the end. In your answer, the number of digits after the decimal point should be the same as the total number of digits after the decimal points in all the numbers being multiplied.

Examples

① 2.73×18

> Multiply as you would whole numbers.

$$273$$
$$\times \quad 18$$
$$\overline{2730}$$
$$2184$$
$$\overline{4914}$$

> Then, count the digits after the decimal point in the numbers being multiplied and transfer to answer.

$2.73 \times 18 = 49.14$

② Therefore $2.73 \times 18 = 49.14$

17.5×9.61

> Multiply as you would whole numbers.

$$175$$
$$\times \quad 961$$
$$\overline{157500}$$
$$10500$$
$$\underline{\quad 175}$$
$$\overline{168175}$$

> Then, count the digits after the decimal point in the numbers being multiplied and transfer to answer.

$17.5 \times 9.61 = 168.175$

Therefore $17.5 \times 9.61 = 168.175$

Decimals

Division of Decimal Numbers by Powers of 10

Division of decimals by powers of 10 is the reverse of multiplying decimal numbers by powers of 10. With division all the digits move a certain number of place values to the right. When you do this your number becomes smaller.

Examples

① 46.3 ÷ 10 = 4.63

Digits move one place value to the right and the number becomes 10 times smaller.

② 3.615 ÷ 100 = 0.03615

Digits move two place values to the right and the number becomes 100 times smaller.

③ 473.2 ÷ 1000 = 0.4732

Digits move three place values to the right and the number becomes 1000 times smaller.

Division of Positive Numbers by Decimal Numbers between 0 and 1

If you divide any positive number by a decimal number between 0 and 1 the answer is always bigger than the positive number you started with.

Examples

① 10 ÷ 0.5 = 20

② 5 ÷ 0.4 = 12.5

③ 471 ÷ 0.01 = 47 100

Division of Decimal Numbers by Whole and Decimal Numbers

Division of a decimal number by a whole number is the same as the division of whole numbers. The only exception is that you must remember to take the decimal point up to your answer.

Example

13.2 ÷ 6

Divide as you would whole numbers

$$
\begin{array}{r}
2.2 \\
6\overline{)13.2} \\
12 \\
\hline
1\ 2 \\
1\ 2 \\
\hline
0
\end{array}
$$

Remember to take the decimal point up to the answer

Therefore **13.2 ÷ 6 = 2.2**

Division of a decimal number by another decimal number is slightly more tricky. Before you start, multiply both numbers by 10, 100, etc. until the number doing the dividing is a whole number. The process from now on is the same as the example above.

Example

4.368 ÷ 0.56

Multiply both numbers by 100 to make the number doing the dividing a whole number.
4.368 × 100 = 436.8, 0.56 × 100 = 56
Divide as you would whole numbers.

$$
\begin{array}{r}
7.8 \\
56\overline{)436.8} \\
392 \\
\hline
4\ 4\ 8 \\
4\ 4\ 8 \\
\hline
0
\end{array}
$$

Remember to take the decimal point up to the answer

Therefore **4.368 ÷ 0.56 = 7.8**

Number Properties

Types of Number

Numbers can be described in many ways. Below is a summary of the types of number that you should know.

Even Numbers

Even numbers are numbers which can be divided exactly by 2. The first ten even numbers in order are…

2, 4, 6, 8, 10, 12, 14, 16, 18, 20

Odd Numbers

Since all whole numbers are either even or odd, then odd numbers are those that cannot be divided exactly by 2.

The first ten odd numbers in order are…

1, 3, 5, 7, 9, 11, 13, 15, 17, 19

Factors (Divisors)

The factors (or divisors) of a number are those whole numbers which divide exactly into it. All numbers, with the exception of square numbers (see page 13), have an even number of factors.

An easy way to find the factors of a number is to look for pairs of numbers that multiply to give that number.

> **Example**
>
> The factors of **10** are **1, 2, 5, 10**
>
> (since 1 × 10 = 10, 2 × 5 = 10)
>
> The factors of **24** are **1, 2, 3, 4, 6, 8, 12, 24**
>
> (since 1 × 24 = 24, 2 × 12 = 24, 3 × 8 = 24, 4 × 6 = 24)

Square numbers have an odd number of factors.

> **Example**
>
> The factors of **16** are **1, 2, 4, 8, 16**
>
> (since 1 × 16 = 16, 2 × 8 = 16, 4 × 4 = 16)
>
> The factors of **36** are **1, 2, 3, 4, 6, 9, 12, 18, 36**
>
> (since 1 × 36 = 36, 2 × 18 = 36, 3 × 12 = 36, 4 × 9 = 36, 6 × 6 = 36)

Multiples

The multiples of a number are those numbers that can be divided exactly by it. To put it simply, they are the numbers found in the 'times' tables.

> **Examples**
>
> The multiples of **5** are **5, 10, 15, 20, 25**, etc.
>
> The multiples of **8** are **8, 16, 24, 32, 40**, etc.

Prime Numbers

Prime numbers are numbers which have only two factors: 1 and the number itself. The first ten prime numbers are…

2, 3, 5, 7, 11, 13, 17, 19, 23, 29

The only even prime number is 2 since all even numbers after this have 2 as a factor, which rules them out as prime numbers.

Reciprocals

The reciprocal of a number is '1 over that number'.

> **Examples**
>
> **1** The reciprocal of 4 is '1 over 4' = $\frac{1}{4}$
>
> **2** The reciprocal of 0.2 is '1 over 0.2'
>
> $$= \frac{1}{0.2} \overset{\times 10}{\underset{\times 10}{}} = \frac{10}{2} = 5$$
>
> **3** The reciprocal of $\frac{2}{3}$ is '1 over $\frac{2}{3}$'
>
> $$= \frac{1}{\left(\frac{2}{3}\right)} = 1 \div \frac{2}{3} = 1 \times \frac{3}{2} = \frac{3}{2} = 1\frac{1}{2}$$
>
> **4** The reciprocal of $\frac{a}{b}$ is $\frac{b}{a}$

Any non-zero number multiplied by its reciprocal is always equal to 1.

> **Examples**
>
> **1** $4 \times \frac{1}{4} = 1$
>
> **2** $0.2 \times 5 = 1$
>
> **3** $\frac{2}{3} \times \frac{3}{2} = 1$

Zero has no reciprocal because anything divided by zero is undefined.

Number Properties

Prime Factor Form

The prime factors of a number are those prime numbers that divide exactly into it. When a number is expressed as a product of its prime factors it is said to be written in prime factor form. To find the prime factor form of a number, try to divide your number by the lowest prime number (i.e. 2). If it works, keep repeating until it will not divide exactly. Then try the next prime number up, and continue until you have an answer of 1. This process is called **prime number decomposition**.

Examples

1 Write **24** in prime factor form.

2	24
2	12
2	6
3	3
	1

So, $24 = 2 \times 2 \times 2 \times 3 = 2^3 \times 3$

2 Write **420** in prime factor form.

2	420
2	210
3	105
5	35
7	7
	1

So, $420 = 2 \times 2 \times 3 \times 5 \times 7 = 2^2 \times 3 \times 5 \times 7$

Alternatively, a prime factor tree can be used to work out the prime factors of a number.

Example

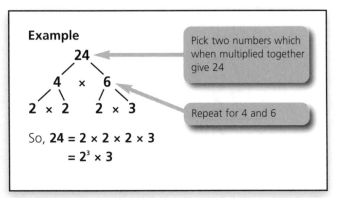

Pick two numbers which when multiplied together give 24

Repeat for 4 and 6

So, $24 = 2 \times 2 \times 2 \times 3$
$= 2^3 \times 3$

Highest Common Factor

The highest common factor (HCF) of two (or more) numbers is the highest number that divides exactly into both (or all of) the numbers. To find the HCF, express your numbers in prime factor form and then select only the prime factors that are common to both numbers.

Example
What is the HCF of **24** and **90**?

First express **24** and **90** in prime factor form...

$24 = 2 \times 2 \times \boxed{2 \times 3}$
$90 = \boxed{2 \times 3} \times 3 \times 5$

... and then select prime factors that are common to both numbers.

HCF of 24 and 90 = $2 \times 3 = 6$

Lowest (Least) Common Multiple

The lowest (least) common multiple (LCM) of two or more numbers is the lowest number that is a multiple of all the numbers. You can use prime number decomposition to find the LCM.

Example
What is the LCM of **8** and **10**?

Write down the multiples of each number...

The multiples of **8** are: **8, 16, 24, 32, ⑷0,
48, 56, 64, 72, 80 and so on...**
The multiples of **10** are: **10, 20, 30, ④0,
50, 60, 70, 80, 90, 100 and so on...**

... and then select the lowest multiple that is common.

LCM of 8 and 10 is 40
(From the two lists above, 80 is also a multiple that is common. However it is **not** the **lowest**).

Whole Number Calculations

Addition and Subtraction of Whole Numbers

Whenever you add or subtract whole numbers you must line up the digits, one on top of the other, in place value order.

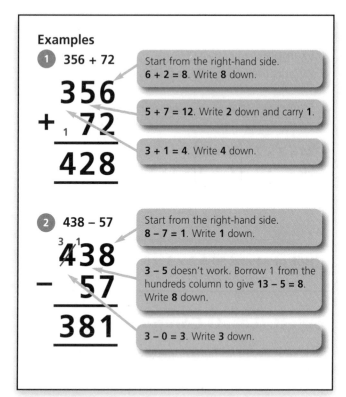

Examples

1 356 + 72

$$\begin{array}{r} 356 \\ +\ _172 \\ \hline 428 \end{array}$$

Start from the right-hand side. **6 + 2 = 8**. Write **8** down.

5 + 7 = 12. Write **2** down and carry **1**.

3 + 1 = 4. Write **4** down.

2 438 − 57

$$\begin{array}{r} \overset{3}{4}\overset{1}{3}8 \\ -\ 57 \\ \hline 381 \end{array}$$

Start from the right-hand side. **8 − 7 = 1**. Write **1** down.

3 − 5 doesn't work. Borrow 1 from the hundreds column to give **13 − 5 = 8**. Write **8** down.

3 − 0 = 3. Write **3** down.

Multiplication and Division of Whole Numbers by Powers of 10

To multiply a whole number by a power of 10, e.g. 10(10^1), 100(10^2), 1000(10^3), all you have to do is move all the digits a certain number of place values to the left. The number of place values moved is equal to the power (number of zeros). When you do this your number becomes bigger.

Example

1 36 × 10 = **360**

2 36 × 100 = **3600**

3 36 × 1000 = **36 000**

To divide a whole number by a power of 10 you move all the digits a certain number of places to the right. The number of places moved is equal to the power (number of zeros). When you do this your number becomes smaller.

Example

1 36 ÷ 10 = **3.6**

2 36 ÷ 100 = **0.36**

3 36 ÷ 1000 = **0.036**

Long Multiplication and Long Division of Whole Numbers

To be successful at long multiplication and long division you need to know the multiplication or 'times' tables.

Examples

1 364 × 14

$$\begin{array}{r} 364 \\ \times\ 14 \\ \hline 3640 \\ 1\overset{2}{4}\overset{1}{5}6 \\ \hline 5096 \end{array}$$

- **14 = 10 + 4**.
- Do the **364 × 10** first. Remember to put a '**0**' down as you would if you multiplied any whole number by **10**.
- Do the **364 × 4** multiplication.
- Add the two multiplications together.

2 312 ÷ 12

$$\begin{array}{r} 26 \\ 12\overline{)312} \\ 24\downarrow \\ \hline 72 \\ 72 \\ \hline 0 \end{array}$$

- **12** does not divide into **3** so move on.
- **12** into **31** goes **2** times. **12 × 2 = 24**. Write **24** below **31** and subtract to give **7**.
- Bring down the **2**. **12** into **72** goes **6** times. **12 × 6 = 72**.

What are Integers?

Integers are whole numbers, including those which are less than zero. Above zero the numbers are positive although we don't write a + (plus) in front of them. Below zero the numbers are negative and these must have a - (minus) written in front of them. When you use positive and negative numbers, zero is the fixed point on the scale. All numbers relate to this point.

A number line (which can be horizontal or vertical) can be a very useful aid for you to understand positive and negative numbers.

Positive and negative numbers are often used in everyday life, e.g. to show temperatures above and below freezing or financial gain and loss.

A Number Line

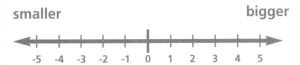

A Bank Statement Showing Deposits and Withdrawals.

LONSDALE BUILDING SOCIETY

Date	Description	Deposit	Withdrawal	Balance
11/12/10				£226.30
12/12/10	The Toy Shop		-£49.99	£176.31
13/12/10	Gas Bill		-£21.03	£155.28
14/12/10	Cheque	£25.00		£180.28
16/12/10	La Trattoria		-£32.98	£147.30
19/12/10	Rent		-£260.00	-£112.70

Ordering Integers

Ordering integers means rearranging a series of positive and negative numbers in either ascending (lowest to highest) or descending (highest to lowest) order.

The simplest way is to collect all the negative and positive numbers together in two separate groups. If you need to you can then use a number line to order the numbers.

Example
Rearrange the following temperatures in ascending order:
7°C, -1°C, 2°C, 5°C, -4°C, -2°C, 3°C, -8°C

Collect the negative and positive numbers together in two separate groups and order using a number line…

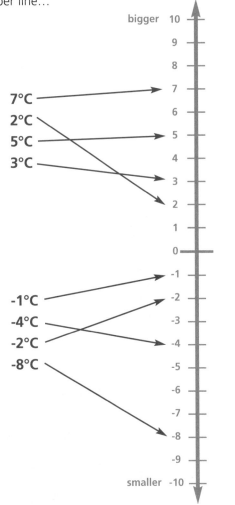

… to give us the temperatures in ascending order:
-8°C, -4°C, -2°C, -1°C, 2°C, 3°C, 5°C, 7°C

Integers

Addition and Subtraction of Integers

When you are adding or subtracting integers, you can draw a number line to help you. Positive numbers are counted to the right of the number line and negative numbers to the left.

Examples

1. At 6pm the temperature in Manchester was 6°C. By 10pm it had fallen by 8°C. The temperature at 10pm is therefore **6°C – 8°C**. On a number line this calculation can be shown by starting at 6 and then counting 8 to the left.

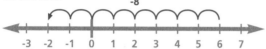

6°C – 8°C **= -2°C**

2. The temperature had fallen a further 6°C by 1am. On a number line this can be shown by starting at -2 and counting 6 places to the left.

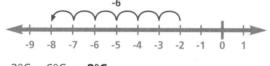

-2°C – 6°C **= -8°C**

Manchester
● 6°C

Multiplication and Division of Integers

When you are multiplying or dividing a pair of integers, ignore any signs and multiply or divide the two numbers to get the number part of the answer. If the numbers have **the same** signs the answer is **positive**, whereas if the numbers have **different** signs the answer is **negative**. This table shows all the possibilities:

Multiplication of Integers	Division of Integers
+ × + = +	+ ÷ + = +
- × - = +	- ÷ - = +
+ × - = -	+ ÷ - = -
- × + = -	- ÷ + = -

Examples

1. 6×-7
   = -42

2. -12×8
   = -96

3. -11×-5
   = 55

4. $\dfrac{75}{-5}$
   = -15

5. $\dfrac{-200}{40}$
   = -5

6. $\dfrac{-99}{-11}$
   = 9

Powers & Roots

Understanding Powers

Powers or indices show that a number is to be multiplied by itself a certain number of times.

$$4^2$$

The power or index

$4 \times 4 = 4^2$ **(4 squared)**
$4 \times 4 \times 4 = 4^3$ **(4 cubed)**
$4 \times 4 \times 4 \times 4 = 4^4$ **(4 to the power 4)**
$4 \times 4 \times 4 \times 4 \times 4 = 4^5$ **(4 to the power 5)**
… and so on

Square Numbers

Numbers obtained by squaring a number are called square numbers.

The first four square numbers are…

1	**4**	**9**	**16**
$(1^2 = 1 \times 1)$	$(2^2 = 2 \times 2)$	$(3^2 = 3 \times 3)$	$(4^2 = 4 \times 4)$

$2^2=$	$3^2=$	$4^2=$	$5^2=$	$10^2=$
4	9	16	25	100

Cube Numbers

Numbers obtained by cubing a number are called cube numbers.

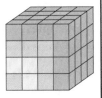

The first four cube numbers are…

1	**8**	**27**	**64**
$(1^3 = 1 \times 1 \times 1)$	$(2^3 = 2 \times 2 \times 2)$	$(3^3 = 3 \times 3 \times 3)$	$(4^3 = 4 \times 4 \times 4)$

$2^3=$	$3^3=$	$4^3=$	$5^3=$	$10^3=$
8	27	64	125	1000

You may be asked to find the value of an expression involving powers without using a calculator.

> **Example**
> Calculate the value of $\mathbf{2^2 \times 3^3}$
> $2^2 \times 3^3 = (2 \times 2) \times (3 \times 3 \times 3) = 4 \times 27 = \mathbf{108}$

Powers of 10

Large numbers can often be written more easily by using a power of 10.

$10^1 = 10$ **(ten)**
$10^2 = 100$ **(one hundred)**
$10^3 = 1000$ **(one thousand)**
$10^4 = 10\,000$ **(ten thousand)**
$10^5 = 100\,000$ **(one hundred thousand)**
$10^6 = 1\,000\,000$ **(one million)**

Powers of Negative Numbers

Great care is needed when working out powers of negative numbers. If you are in any doubt refer back to page 12 for the multiplication of integers.

> **Examples**
> **1** $(-4)^2 = -4 \times -4 = \mathbf{16}$
> (since a 'minus' times a 'minus' is equal to a 'plus')
>
> **2** $(-4)^3 = -4 \times -4 \times -4 = \mathbf{-64}$
> (the first two 'minuses' give a 'plus'. This 'plus' times a 'minus' then gives a 'minus').

Powers & Roots

Rules of Indices

Indices is another word for Powers.

1 A number to a power of 1 is the number itself.

$3^1 = 3$

$10^1 = 10$

2 Any non-zero number to the power of 0 is equal to 1

$3^0 = $ **1**

$10^0 = $ **1**

3 When multiplying, powers of the same number are added.

$3^5 \times 3^2 = 3^{5+2} = $ **3^7**

$10^3 \times 10 = 10^{3+1} = $ **10^4**

4 When dividing, powers of the same number are subtracted.

$3^5 \div 3^2 = 3^{5-2} = $ **3^3**

$10^3 \div 10 = 10^{3-1} = $ **10^2**

Examples

1 Simplify $3^5 \times 3^7$

$= 3^{5+7}$

$= 3^{12}$

2 Simplify $\dfrac{4^5}{4}$

$= 4^{5-1}$

$= 4^4$

3 Evaluate $\dfrac{3^4 \times 3^7}{3^8}$

$= \dfrac{3^{4+7}}{3^8}$ ⟵ – Do the multiplication first.
– Then the division.

$= 3^{11-8}$

$= 3^3$

$= 27$

4 Evaluate $\dfrac{7^4 \times 7^5}{7 \times 7^8}$

$= \dfrac{7^{4+5}}{7^{1+8}}$

$= \dfrac{7^9}{7^9}$

$= 7^0$

$= 1$ ⟵ Since any number to the power of 0 is equal to 1

Square Roots

You know that **$4^2 = 16$** and **$(-4)^2 = 16$**

It follows that 4 and -4 are both **square roots** of 16.

If $x^2 = $ **16** then $x = \pm\sqrt{16} = $ **±4**

An important point is that the symbol $\sqrt{}$ is used to represent the positive square root, i.e. $\sqrt{16} = 4$.

Since $a^2 \geqslant 0$ for any value of a, it follows that we can only find the square roots of positive numbers.

You will be expected to be able to recall the square roots of all integer squares from **2^2 (4)** to **15^2 (225)**.

$\sqrt{4}$	=	2		
$\sqrt{9}$	=	3		
$\sqrt{16}$	=	4		
$\sqrt{25}$	=	5		
$\sqrt{36}$	=	6		
$\sqrt{49}$	=	7		
$\sqrt{64}$	=	8		

$\sqrt{81}$	=	9
$\sqrt{100}$	=	10
$\sqrt{121}$	=	11
$\sqrt{144}$	=	12
$\sqrt{169}$	=	13
$\sqrt{196}$	=	14
$\sqrt{225}$	=	15

Cube Roots of Positive Numbers

Finding the cube root of a positive number results in only one root: a positive root.

Examples

1 Since **$4^3 = 4 \times 4 \times 4 = 64$**,

then **4 is the cube root of 64**. Therefore...

$\sqrt[3]{64} = 4$

2 $\sqrt[3]{125} = 5$ (since $5 \times 5 \times 5 = 125$)

3 $\sqrt[3]{1000} = 10$ (since $10 \times 10 \times 10 = 1000$)

Order of Operations

Bidmas

The simplest possible calculation involves only one operation, e.g. an addition or multiplication.

However, when a calculation involves more than one operation, you must carry them out in the order shown here.

BIDMAS

| Brackets | Indices (or power) | Divisions and Multiplications – can be done in any order | Additions and Subtractions – can be done in any order |

Examples

1. $8 + 3 \times 4$

   Do the multiplication first

   $= 8 + 12$

   Then the addition

   $= 20$

2. $\dfrac{(14 + 6)}{-4}$

   Do the addition in the brackets first

   $= \dfrac{20}{-4}$

   Then the division

   $= -5 \ (+ \div - = -)$

3. $4^2 - 2 \times 5$

   Work out the square first

   $= 16 - 2 \times 5$

   Then the multiplication

   $= 16 - 10$

   Then the subtraction

   $= 6$

4. 4×3^2 ← A common mistake is to work out 4×3^2 as $12^2 = 144$.

   Work out the square first

   $= 4 \times 9$

   Then the multiplication

   $= 36$

Use of Brackets

Inserting brackets into a calculation changes the order in which the operations are carried out and this produces different answers.

Examples

1. Here is a calculation without brackets.

   $8 + 3 \times 4 - 2 = 8 + 12 - 2 = 20 - 2 = \mathbf{18}$

   (or 8 + 10)

   If we now insert one pair of brackets into the calculation the possible answers become...

   $(8 + 3) \times 4 - 2 = 11 \times 4 - 2 = 44 - 2 = \mathbf{42}$

   $8 + 3 \times (4 - 2) = 8 + 3 \times 2 = 8 + 6 = \mathbf{14}$

2. The diagram represents part of a garden that is to be paved. The cost of the paving is £15 per m². Calculate the total cost.

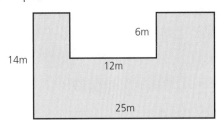

The total cost in £ is given by

$(25 \times 14 - 12 \times 6) \times 15$

$= \mathbf{£4170}$

Enter this on a calculator as it looks written here

Fractions

Understanding Simple Fractions

The diagram shows a whole pizza that has been cut into four equal parts (or slices). Each slice can be described as a fraction of the whole pizza and its value is $\frac{1}{4}$.

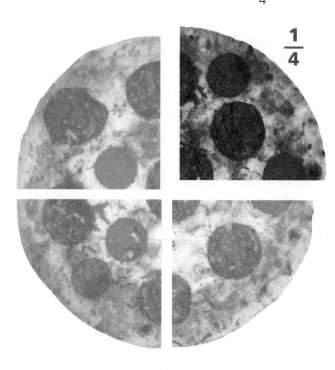

$$\frac{1}{4}$$

The pizza, however, could have been cut into any number of segments, where each segment is a different fraction of the whole pizza (see the diagrams below).

The top number of a fraction is called the **numerator** while the bottom number is called the **denominator**.

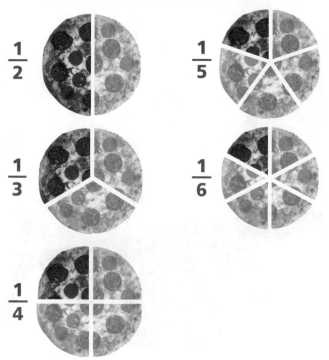

$\frac{1}{2}$ $\frac{1}{5}$

$\frac{1}{3}$ $\frac{1}{6}$

$\frac{1}{4}$

Equivalent Fractions

Equivalent fractions are fractions that are equal. You can build chains of equivalent fractions by multiplying the numerator and denominator in the fraction by the same number.

Examples

① This chain was formed using the two times table.

$$\overset{\times 2}{\frac{1}{4}} = \overset{\times 2}{\frac{2}{8}} = \overset{\times 2}{\frac{4}{16}} = \frac{8}{32}$$

② This chain was formed using the three times table.

$$\overset{\times 3}{\frac{1}{5}} = \overset{\times 3}{\frac{3}{15}} = \overset{\times 3}{\frac{9}{45}} = \frac{27}{135}$$

Cancelling Fractions

You can also divide the numerator and denominator in a fraction by the same number. Chains of equivalent fractions that are cancelled down using division always come to an end when the fraction is expressed in its simplest form, i.e. lowest terms.

Examples

① $$\overset{\div 3}{\frac{18}{27}} = \overset{\div 3}{\frac{6}{9}} = \frac{2}{3}$$

② $$\overset{\div 3}{\frac{45}{60}} = \overset{\div 5}{\frac{15}{20}} = \frac{3}{4}$$

③ $$\overset{\div 2}{\frac{100}{140}} = \overset{\div 2}{\frac{50}{70}} = \overset{\div 5}{\frac{25}{35}} = \frac{5}{7}$$

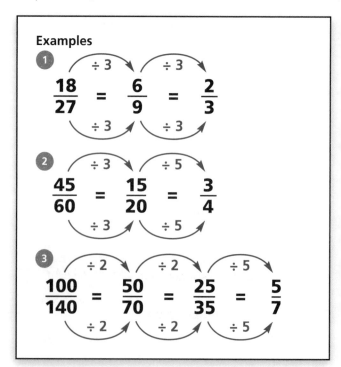

Fractions

Ordering Fractions

To order fractions, write each fraction with a common denominator. If you are unsure, choose the lowest common multiple of the denominators given. You can then order the fractions by the 'size' of the numerators.

Example

Arrange $\frac{9}{10}$, $\frac{4}{5}$, $\frac{7}{8}$ in ascending order.

Firstly write each fraction with a common denominator. The lowest common multiple of 10, 5 and 8 is 40.

Therefore…

$$\frac{9}{10} = \frac{36}{40} \quad \frac{4}{5} = \frac{32}{40} \quad \frac{7}{8} = \frac{35}{40}$$

(×4) (×8) (×5)

Now we can compare the numerators and arrange the fractions in ascending (lowest to highest) order.

In ascending order they are: $\frac{4}{5}$, $\frac{7}{8}$, $\frac{9}{10}$

When you have fractions with common denominators it is possible to find other fractions that lie between these fractions.

For example, from above $\frac{4}{5} = \frac{32}{40}$ and $\frac{7}{8} = \frac{35}{40}$. It should be obvious that we can write two other fractions with denominator 40 which are greater than $\frac{4}{5}$ but less than $\frac{7}{8}$. They would be $\frac{33}{40}$ and $\frac{34}{40}$, the later cancels down to $\frac{17}{20}$.

Improper Fractions and Mixed Numbers

Some fractions are known as improper because they are 'top heavy', i.e. the top number is bigger than the bottom number, e.g. $\frac{5}{4}$ is 'top heavy'. Improper fractions need simplifying into a mixed number so that they are easier to read and understand.

If we go back to our pizza on the previous page, then $\frac{5}{4}$ would be one whole pizza cut into four slices, plus one extra slice from another pizza.

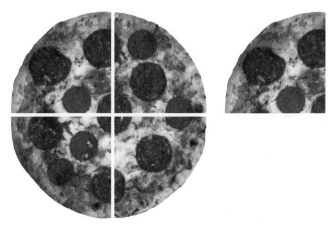

In other words…

$$\frac{5}{4} = \frac{4}{4} + \frac{1}{4} = 1\frac{1}{4}$$

Examples

1. $\frac{13}{5} = \frac{5}{5} + \frac{5}{5} + \frac{3}{5} = \mathbf{2\frac{3}{5}}$

2. $\frac{19}{6} = \frac{6}{6} + \frac{6}{6} + \frac{6}{6} + \frac{1}{6} = \mathbf{3\frac{1}{6}}$

   $19 \div 6 = \mathbf{3} + \frac{1}{6}$ **left over!**

   The examples above show improper fractions being changed into mixed numbers. The reverse process can also be used to change mixed numbers into improper fractions.

3. $2\frac{3}{5} = \frac{2 \times 5 + 3}{5} = \frac{13}{5}$

Fractions

Addition of Fractions

Two fractions can be added very easily providing they have common denominators.

Example

$\frac{2}{5} = \frac{8}{20}$ $\qquad \frac{2}{5} + \frac{3}{4} \qquad$ $\frac{3}{4} = \frac{15}{20}$

$$= \frac{8}{20} + \frac{15}{20}$$

$$= \frac{23}{20}$$

$$= 1\frac{3}{20}$$

With mixed numbers, add the whole numbers and fractions separately and then combine.

Example

$$2\frac{2}{3} + 3\frac{1}{7}$$

$$= (2 + 3) + \left(\frac{2}{3} + \frac{1}{7}\right)$$

$$= 5 + \left(\frac{14}{21} + \frac{3}{21}\right)$$

$$= 5\frac{17}{21}$$

Subtraction of Fractions

As with addition, two fractions can be subtracted very easily providing they have common denominators.

Example

$\frac{7}{8} = \frac{21}{24}$ $\qquad \frac{7}{8} - \frac{2}{3} \qquad$ $\frac{2}{3} = \frac{16}{24}$

$$= \frac{21}{24} - \frac{16}{24}$$

$$= \frac{5}{24}$$

With mixed numbers, subtract the whole numbers and fractions separately and then combine.

Example

$$4\frac{1}{2} - 1\frac{4}{5}$$

$$= (4 - 1) + \left(\frac{1}{2} - \frac{4}{5}\right)$$

$$= 3 + \left(\frac{5}{10} - \frac{8}{10}\right)$$

$$= 3 + \left(-\frac{3}{10}\right)$$

$$= 3 - \frac{3}{10} = 2\frac{7}{10}$$

Alternatively, you can use improper fractions.

$$4\frac{1}{2} - 1\frac{4}{5}$$

$$= \frac{9}{2} - \frac{9}{5}$$

$$= \frac{45}{10} - \frac{18}{10}$$

$$= \frac{27}{10}$$

$$= 2\frac{7}{10}$$

Multiplication and Division of Fractions

To multiply two fractions, multiply the two numerators together and multiply the two denominators together.

Example

$$\frac{2}{3} \times \frac{4}{5} = \frac{2\times4}{3\times5} = \frac{8}{15}$$

Division of two fractions is the same as multiplication, except that you turn the second fraction (that is doing the dividing) upside down and change the division sign to a multiplication sign.

Example

$$\frac{2}{3} \div \frac{4}{5} = \frac{2}{3} \times \frac{5}{4} = \frac{2\times5}{3\times4} = \frac{10}{12} = \frac{5}{6}$$

To multiply or divide mixed numbers you have to convert them to improper fractions first.

Example

1 $\quad 2\frac{1}{2} \times 1\frac{1}{6} = \frac{5}{2} \times \frac{7}{6}$

$$= \frac{5\times7}{2\times6}$$

$$= \frac{35}{12}$$

$$= 2\frac{11}{12}$$

2 $\quad 1\frac{1}{3} \div 3\frac{1}{2} = \frac{4}{3} \div \frac{7}{2}$

$$= \frac{4}{3} \times \frac{2}{7}$$

$$= \frac{4\times2}{3\times7}$$

$$= \frac{8}{21}$$

To multiply or divide a fraction by an integer, convert the integer to an improper fraction. For example, 4 as an improper fraction is $\frac{4}{1}$. You can then do the multiplication or division as normal.

Example

1 $\quad \frac{4}{7} \times 3 = \frac{4}{7} \times \frac{3}{1}$

$$= \frac{4\times3}{7\times1}$$

$$= \frac{12}{7}$$

$$= 1\frac{5}{7}$$

2 $\quad \frac{2}{3} \div 10 = \frac{2}{3} \div \frac{10}{1}$

$$= \frac{2}{3} \times \frac{1}{10}$$

$$= \frac{2\times1}{3\times10}$$

$$= \frac{2}{30}$$

$$= \frac{1}{15}$$

Fractions

Calculating a Fraction of a Quantity

To find a fraction of any quantity, you have to multiply the fraction by the quantity. In other words, 'of' means 'times' or 'multiply' (×).

Examples

1. Calculate $\frac{4}{5}$ of 60kg.

$$\frac{4}{5} \text{ of 60kg} = \frac{4}{5} \times 60 \qquad \text{'of' means '×'}$$

$$= \frac{4}{5} \times \frac{60}{1} = \frac{240}{5} = \textbf{48kg}$$

Alternatively: $\frac{4}{\cancel{5}_1} \times \frac{\cancel{60}^{12}}{1} = \frac{48}{1} = \textbf{48kg}$

2. A brand new car costing £9000 will lose $\frac{1}{5}$ of its value in the first year. What is the value of the car after the first year? Before we can calculate its value we need to calculate the loss.

$$\text{Loss} = \frac{1}{5} \text{ of £9000} = \frac{1}{5} \times 9000 = \frac{9000}{5}$$

'of' means '×'

$$= \frac{9000}{5} = \text{£1800}$$

Value of car after the first year

$$= \text{£9000} - \text{£1800} = \textbf{£7200}.$$

OR $1 - \frac{1}{5} = \frac{4}{5}$ of value after first year
$= \text{£9000} \times \frac{4}{5} = \frac{36\,000}{5} = \textbf{£7200}$

3. A marathon runner covers a distance of $12\frac{1}{2}$ miles in $1\frac{1}{4}$ hours on a training run. What is his average speed?

$$\boxed{\textbf{Average speed} = \frac{\textbf{Distance}}{\textbf{Time}}}$$

$$= 12\frac{1}{2} \div 1\frac{1}{4}$$

$$= \frac{25}{2} \div \frac{5}{4}$$

$$= \frac{\cancel{25}^5}{\cancel{2}_1} \times \frac{\cancel{4}^2}{\cancel{5}_1}$$

$$= \frac{10}{1}$$

$$= \textbf{10 miles per hour (mph)}$$

Expressing One Quantity as a Fraction of Another Quantity

Firstly, you must make sure that both quantities are in the same units. Then, to express the relationship as a fraction, the first quantity becomes the numerator (top number) and the second quantity becomes the denominator (bottom number). If need be, write the fraction in its lowest terms.

Examples

1. Write 30 out of 120 as a fraction.

$$30 \text{ out of } 120 = \frac{30}{120} = \frac{\textbf{1}}{\textbf{4}}$$

2. Express 36 seconds as a fraction of 2 minutes. Both quantities must be in the same units, so change 2 minutes into seconds.
2 minutes = 2 × 60s = 120s, so…

$$36\text{s as a fraction of } 120\text{s} = \frac{36}{120} = \frac{\textbf{3}}{\textbf{10}}$$

Percentages

Understanding Simple Percentages

Percentages are used in everyday life, from pay rises to price reductions. This helps us to make easy comparisons. When you understand the basics of percentages they are even easier to calculate than decimals or fractions.

Percentages focus on the whole being equal to one hundred, i.e. the whole is one hundred percent. So, if someone gives you 50% of a whole pizza, this tells you the 'number of parts per 100' you have, e.g. 50% is '50 parts per 100' or $\frac{50}{100}$.

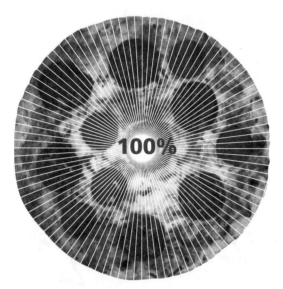

100%

10% 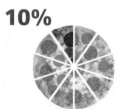	**40%** 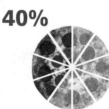
20%	**50%**
30% 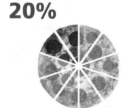	**etc.**

Calculating a Percentage of a Quantity

Examples

① Calculate 40% of 50cm.

> 40% means 40 parts per 100 or $\frac{40}{100}$ and 'of' means 'times' or 'multiply' (×).

$$40\% \text{ of } 50\text{cm} = \frac{40}{100} \times 50 = \frac{40 \times 50}{100}$$
$$= \textbf{20cm}$$

② Calculate 15% of £4.80.
Give your answer in pence.

$$£4.80 = 4.80 \times 100\text{p} = \textbf{480p}$$

> 15% means 15 parts out of 100 or $\frac{15}{100}$ and 'of' means 'times' (×).

$$15\% \text{ of } 480\text{p} = \frac{15}{100} \times 480$$
$$= \frac{\overset{3}{\cancel{15}} \times \cancel{480}^{24}}{\cancel{100}_{\cancel{5}_1}}$$
$$= \frac{72}{1}$$
$$= \textbf{72p}$$

Expressing One Quantity as a Percentage of Another Quantity

Make sure that both quantities are in the same units. Firstly, express one quantity as a fraction of the other, where the first quantity becomes the numerator (top number) and the second quantity becomes the denominator (bottom number). Then multiply the fraction by 100%.

Examples

① Write 18 out of 30 as a percentage.

$$18 \text{ out of } 30 = \frac{18}{30} \times 100\%$$
$$= \frac{\overset{3}{\cancel{18}} \times \cancel{100}^{20}}{\cancel{30}_{\cancel{8}_1}} = \textbf{60\%}$$

② Express 30cm as a percentage of 3m. Both quantities must be in the same units, so change 3m into centimetres.
3m = 3 × 100cm = 300cm, so...

$$30\text{cm as a \% of } 300\text{cm} = \frac{30}{300} \times 100\%$$
$$= \frac{\cancel{30}^{1} \times 100}{\cancel{300}_{10}} = \textbf{10\%}$$

Percentages

Mental methods

It's very useful to know the following equivalents as, with a bit of practice, you can use them to work out percentages of amounts without a calculator.

$10\% = \frac{1}{10}$

$50\% = \frac{1}{2}$

$25\% = \frac{1}{4}$

$75\% = \frac{3}{4}$

$12\frac{1}{2}\% = \frac{1}{8}$

$33\frac{1}{3}\% = \frac{1}{3}$

For example, since 10% = 1/10, to find 10% of any amount you just divide it by 10.

So, 10% of 640 = 64 and 10% of £37 = £3.70

If you need 20% of an amount, find 10% and then double it.

If you need 5% of an amount, find 10% and halve it.

Examples
Calculate the following percentages without using a calculator.

1 30% of £36

10% of £36 = £3.60
30% of £36 = 3 × £3.60 = **£10.80**

2 5% of £42

10% of £42 = £4.20

5% of £42 = $\frac{£4.20}{2}$ = £2.10

15% of £42 = **£6.30** (15% = 10% + 5%)

3 12½% of £80

$12\frac{1}{2}\%$ of £80 = $\frac{£80}{8}$

= **£10**

4 25% of £14

25% of £14 = $\frac{£14}{4}$ (Or you can halve it twice)

= **£3.50**

5 $33\frac{1}{3}\%$ of 120kg

$33\frac{1}{3}\%$ of 120kg = $\frac{120kg}{3}$ = **40kg**

Increasing by a percentage

There are many situations where we need to increase an amount by a percentage. For example, a pay rise, a gain in height, a price increase due to inflation or the total cost of a product including VAT.

Example
A standard box of breakfast cereal weighs 500g. Special boxes contain an extra 25%. Calculate the weight of a special box of cereal.

> Firstly calculate the increase in weight.

25% of 500g = $\frac{25}{100}$ × 500g = $\frac{25 \times 500}{100}$ = **125g**

> Then add it to the weight of a standard box of cereal.

Weight of special box = 500g + 125g = 625g

An alternative method would be as follows: A standard box of cereal is to be increased by 25%. If a standard box is 100%, a special box will be:

100% + 25% = 125%

125% = $\frac{125}{100}$ = 1.25

In other words, the weight of a special box is 1.25 times the weight of a standard box.
Weight of special box = 500 × 1.25 = 625g

1.25 is called a **multiplier**. Multiplying any amount by 1.25 will increase it by 25%.

Reducing by a percentage

Some examples of reducing by a percentage are; a weight loss, a temperature drop, a reduction in reported crime or a price reduction in a sale.

Example
A coat priced at £56 is reduced by 20% in a sale. What is the sale price?

10% of £56 = £5.60
20% of £56 = 2 × £5.60 = £11.20

Sale price = £56 – £11.20 = **£44.80**

Alternatively, you can use a multiplier.
100% – 20% = 80% so the multiplier = $\frac{80}{100}$ = 0.8

Sale price = £56 × 0.8 = **£44.80**

Percentages

VAT

The rate of VAT (Value Added Tax) varies from time-to-time but its current value is 17.5%. VAT is added to the price of products and services to give the total price that is to be paid.

Example

A computer is priced at £340 + VAT. What is the total price of the computer?

10% of £340 = £34
5% of £340 = £17   (£34 ÷ 2 = £17)
2.5% of £340 = £8.50   (£17 ÷ 2 = £8.50)
17.5% of £340 = £59.50   (10% + 5% + 2.5%)

The total price is £340 + £59.50 = **£399.50**

An alternative approach is to use a multiplier.

100% + 17.5% = 117.5%

$$= \frac{117.5}{100}$$

$$= 1.175$$

Total price = £340 × 1.175 = **£399.50**

Further Use of Multipliers

Multipliers are probably best used when you have a calculator available. The table below shows some examples of how multipliers may be used.

Calculation	%	Multiplier
Find 37% of an amount	37	0.37
Find 8% of an amount	8	0.08
Find 26.4% of an amount	26.4	0.264
Increase an amount by 16%	116	1.16
Increase an amount by 7%	107	1.07
Reduce an amount by 12%	88	0.88
Reduce an amount by 95%	5	0.05

- When the percentage to be calculated is less than 100% the multiplier lies between 0 and 1.
- When the percentage to be calculated is more than 100% the multiplier is greater than 1.

Income Tax

The amount of income tax that you pay is calculated as a percentage of your earnings once any allowances have been deducted.

Example

Jo earns £16 000 per year. She doesn't pay tax on the first £6035 of her earnings but pays tax at 20% on the remainder. How much tax does Jo pay over the year?

Jo pays tax on £16000 − £6035 = £9965

Jo pays 20% of £9965 in tax.

10% of £9965 = £996.50
20% of £9965 = 2 × £996.50 = **£1993**

Jo pays **£1993** in tax over the year.

Alternatively, the multiplier for 20% = 0.2

0.2 × £9965 = **£1993**

Fractions, Decimals & Percentages

Below is a summary of how to convert between fractions, decimals and percentages. You may start at any of the three points. Follow the charts and see how you can move from one system to another by following simple rules.

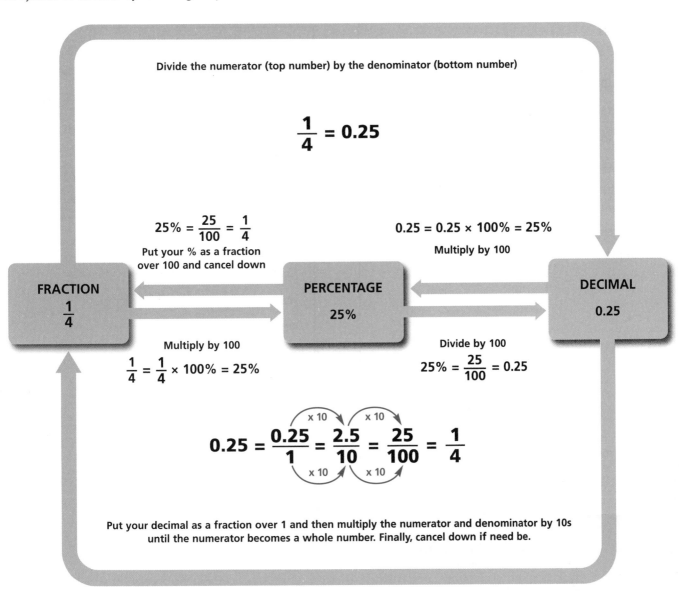

Divide the numerator (top number) by the denominator (bottom number)

$$\frac{1}{4} = 0.25$$

$25\% = \frac{25}{100} = \frac{1}{4}$

Put your % as a fraction over 100 and cancel down

$0.25 = 0.25 \times 100\% = 25\%$

Multiply by 100

FRACTION	PERCENTAGE	DECIMAL
$\frac{1}{4}$	25%	0.25

Multiply by 100

$\frac{1}{4} = \frac{1}{4} \times 100\% = 25\%$

Divide by 100

$25\% = \frac{25}{100} = 0.25$

$$0.25 = \frac{0.25}{1} = \frac{2.5}{10} = \frac{25}{100} = \frac{1}{4}$$

(× 10, × 10)

Put your decimal as a fraction over 1 and then multiply the numerator and denominator by 10s until the numerator becomes a whole number. Finally, cancel down if need be.

$$\frac{2}{5} = 0.4$$

$40\% = \frac{40}{100} = \frac{2}{5}$ $0.4 = 0.4 \times 100\% = 40\%$

FRACTION	PERCENTAGE	DECIMAL
$\frac{2}{5}$	40%	0.4

$\frac{2}{5} = \frac{2}{5} \times 100\% = 40\%$ $40\% = \frac{40}{100} = 0.4$

$$0.4 = \frac{0.4}{1} = \frac{4}{10} = \frac{2}{5}$$

$$\frac{1}{2} = 0.5$$

$50\% = \frac{50}{100} = \frac{5}{10} = \frac{1}{2}$ $0.5 = 0.5 \times 100\% = 50\%$

FRACTION	PERCENTAGE	DECIMAL
$\frac{1}{2}$	50%	0.5

$\frac{1}{2} = \frac{1}{2} \times 100\% = 50\%$ $50\% = \frac{50}{100} = 0.5$

$$0.5 = \frac{0.5}{1} = \frac{5}{10} = \frac{1}{2}$$

Fractions, Decimals and Percentages

Fractions

Fractions with the same denominator (bottom number) may be easily compared.

> **Examples**
>
> **1** $\frac{4}{7}$ is more than $\frac{3}{7}$ because 4 is more than 3.
>
> We may write this as $\frac{4}{7} > \frac{3}{7}$
>
> **2** $\frac{5}{12}$ is smaller than $\frac{11}{12}$ because 5 is smaller than 11.
>
> We may write this as $\frac{5}{12} < \frac{11}{12}$

Equivalent fractions are needed to compare fractions with different denominators.

> **Example**
>
> Compare $\frac{5}{8}$ and $\frac{13}{24}$.
>
> $$\overset{\times 3}{\frac{5}{8}} = \underset{\times 3}{\frac{15}{24}}$$ So we can now compare $\frac{15}{24}$ and $\frac{13}{24}$.
>
> $\frac{15}{24}$ is more than $\frac{13}{24}$
>
> so $\frac{5}{8}$ is more than $\frac{13}{24}$
>
> We may write this as $\frac{5}{8} > \frac{13}{24}$

Fractions, Decimals and Percentages

To order a list of numbers containing fractions, decimals and percentages it is usually easiest to convert all of them to the same form first.

> **Example**
>
> Write the following in order, starting with the smallest.
>
> 70%, $\frac{4}{5}$, 0.75, 72.8%
>
> Two of the values are given as percentages and the other two values are easily converted.
>
> $$\frac{4}{5} = \frac{4}{5} \times 100\%$$
>
> $$= \frac{4}{\underset{1}{\cancel{5}}} \times \overset{20}{\cancel{100}}\%$$
>
> $$= \mathbf{80\%}$$
>
> > To change either a fraction or a decimal to a percentage, multiply by 100%.
>
> $0.75 = 0.75 \times 100\% = \mathbf{75\%}$.
>
> Writing the percentages in order gives:
>
> **70%, 72.8%, 75%, 80%**
>
> So the original values, in order, are:
>
> **70%, 72.8%, 0.75, $\frac{4}{5}$**

VAT

Value Added Tax or VAT is charged on most goods you buy or any services you receive.

Example

Penny wants to buy this mp3 player priced at £50. How much will it cost her if VAT is charged at a rate of $17\frac{1}{2}$%?

VAT = $17\frac{1}{2}$% of £50

$\quad = 17\frac{1}{2} \times £50$

$\quad$ = **£8.75**

£50 + VAT

Therefore, total cost
$\quad$ = £50 + £8.75
$\quad$ = **£58.75**

Purchasing on Credit

Purchasing on credit is when you pay a deposit on a purchase and then you make a number of repayments spread over a certain period of time.

Example

Jim is buying a car on credit. How much will it cost him altogether?

£6000 or 20% Deposit & 36 monthly repayments of £160

20% deposit = 20% of £6000

$\quad = \dfrac{20}{100} \times 6000 = $ **£1200**

Total cost of repayments = 36 × £160
$\qquad\qquad\qquad\qquad\quad = $ **£5760**

Total cost to Jim = £1200 + £5760 = £6960
(This is £960 more than the cash price but he has spread the cost over 36 months).

Simple Interest

Simple interest is the interest gained on money that is invested and is the same every year.

Example

a) Mr and Mrs Smith have just won £10 000 on the lottery. They decide that they want to invest this money for 2 years. Mr Smith wants to invest the money at 6% simple interest. How much interest will he gain after 2 years?

Interest gained after 1st year

= 6% of £10 000

$= \dfrac{6}{100} \times £10\ 000 = $ **£600**

Interest gained after 2nd year
= £600 (same as 1st year)

Total interest gained
= £600 + £600 = £1200

b) Mr and Mrs Smith put the money in a special account that pays a single interest payment of 33%. Would this be better than 6% simple interest for 5 years?

Interest gained after 5 years
= 33% of £10 000

$= \dfrac{33}{100} \times £10\ 000 = $ **£3300**

This would compare to
5 × £600 = **£3000 simple interest**

So, the single payment of 33% would be the better option.

Everyday Maths

Household Bills

Here is an example of home-owner's electricity bill for one quarter:

> The number of units used is found by subtracting the two meter readings

> 786 units × 7.5 pence per unit = £58.95

Meter Reading				
Present	**Previous**	**Units used**	**Pence per unit**	**Amount**
25081	24295	786	7.5	£58.95
			Quarterly charge	£10.45
		Total charged this quarter excluding VAT		£69.40
			VAT at 5%	£3.47
			Total payable	£72.87

> 5% of £69.40
> $= \frac{5}{100} \times £69.40$
> = £3.47

> You have to pay this regardless of how much electricity you use

> £69.40 + £3.47 = £72.87

Note that VAT is charged at 5% on utilities.

Understanding Tables and Charts

The secret to understanding tables and charts is to identify the relevant data. Once you've done this all you need to use is a bit of 'common sense'.

Example

A rail company operating trains out of Petersfield decides to offer cheap 'Off Peak' fares on services that arrive at London Waterloo after 10am. If a customer who usually catches the 0833 service from Petersfield decides to wait for the first Off Peak train, to take advantage of the offer, what will be the difference in his journey time?

The first thing to do is to identify the relevant data. This is shown in the third and fourth columns of the timetable shown below and has been highlighted for this purpose.

Usual journey time = Arrival Time – Departure Time
= 0939h – 0833h
= 1h 6min

Off Peak journey time = Arrival Time – Departure Time
= 1018h – 0901h

> Remember to calculate hours & minutes separately

= 1h 17min

Difference in time = 1h 17min – 1h 6min
= 11min

Petersfield, Milford, Farncombe, Woking to London Waterloo

Mondays to Fridays

	AN	NW	AN	AN	AN
Petersfield	0752	0811	0833	0901	0928
Liphook	—	—	—	—	—
Haslemere	—	—	—	—	—
Witley	—	—	—	—	—
Milford (Surrey)	0806	0829	0845	0917	0941
Godalming	—	—	—	—	—
Farncombe	0822	0850	0900	0937	0959
Guildford	—	—	—	—	—
Reading	—	—	—	—	—
Woking	0830	0900	0907	0947	1007
Heathrow Airport (T1)	—	—	—	—	—
Clapham Junction	—	—	—	—	—
London Waterloo	0903	0932	0939	1018	1036

Mondays to Fridays

	AN	NW	AN	AN	AN
Petersfield	0949	0956	1019	1049	1055
Liphook	—	—	—	—	—
Haslemere	—	—	—	—	—
Witley	—	—	—	—	—
Milford (Surrey)	1002	1011	1032	1102	1114
Godalming	—	—	—	—	—
Farncombe	1017	1032	1047	1117	1132
Guildford	—	—	—	—	—
Reading	—	—	—	—	—
Woking	1026	1043	1059	1128	1142
Heathrow Airport (T1)	—	—	—	—	—
Clapham Junction	—	—	—	—	—
London Waterloo	1052	1111	1125	1155	1211

Ratio & Proportion

What is a Ratio?

A ratio is a comparison between two or more quantities. The image alongside shows two columns of coins. The first column has ten £1 coins and the second column has six 2p coins. To compare the two sets of coins we can say that the ratio of the number of £1 coins to 2p coins is…

10 to 6 or 10 : 6

Ratios can be cancelled down into their simplest form, just like fractions…

$$÷2 \left(\begin{array}{c} 10 : 6 \\ = 5 : 3 \end{array} \right) ÷2$$

A ratio of **5 : 3** means that for every five £1 coins there are three 2p coins. The above ratio can also be written in the form **1 : n** by dividing both numbers in the ratio by 5…

$$÷5 \left(\begin{array}{c} 5 : 3 \\ = 1 : 0.6 \end{array} \right) ÷5$$

It could be written in the form n : 1 by dividing both numbers in the ratio by 3…

$$÷3 \left(\begin{array}{c} 5 : 3 \\ = 1.\dot{6} : 1 \end{array} \right) ÷3$$

Examples

1 A bag of carrots weighs 300g and a bag of potatoes weighs 1.5kg. Calculate the ratio of weight of carrots to weight of potatoes.

Both quantities must be in the same units.

1.5kg = 1.5 × 1000g = **1500g**

Ratio of weight of carrots to weight of potatoes is as follows:

$$÷300 \left(\begin{array}{c} 300g : 1500g \\ = 1 : 5 \end{array} \right) ÷300$$

2 On a map, a distance of 6km is shown as 3cm. Write the map distance (3cm) to the real distance (6km) as a ratio in its simplest form.

The ratio is 3cm : 6km
= 3cm : 6 × 1000 × 100cm
= 3 : 600 000
= 1 : 200 000

> Make the units the same for both parts of the ratio, then simplify by cancelling the units and any common factors.

Ratios and Fractions

A ratio can be written as a fraction and vice versa.

Examples

1 If $\frac{2}{5}$ of a class are boys what is the ratio of boys to girls? Give your answer in the form 1 : n.

The ratio of boys to girls is as follows:

$$×5 \left(\begin{array}{c} \frac{2}{5} : \frac{3}{5} \\ = 2 : 3 \end{array} \right) ×5$$

Written in the form **1 : n**:

$$×5 \left(\begin{array}{c} 2 : 3 \\ = 1 : 1.5 \end{array} \right) ×5$$

In other words, for any one boy in the class there are one and a half girls.

2 A drink is made by mixing cordial and water in the ratio 1 : 4. What fraction of the drink is cordial?

1 part out of 5 (1 + 4) parts is cordial. The fraction of the drink that is cordial is $\frac{1}{5}$.

3 John mixes concrete by using cement, sand and gravel in the ratio 1 : 2 : 3. What fraction of the mix is sand?

2 parts out of 6 (1 + 2 + 3) parts is sand. The fraction of the cement that is sand is $\frac{2}{6} = \frac{1}{3}$

Ratio & Proportion

Dividing a Quantity in a Given Ratio

Examples

1 £60 is to be divided between Jon and Pat in the ratio 2 : 3. How much money does each one receive?

> We need to divide £60 in the ratio 2 : 3.

The digits in the ratio represent parts. Jon gets 2 parts and Pat gets 3 parts. The total number of parts is **2 + 3 = 5** parts, which is equal to £60. Therefore it follows that…

$$÷5 \left(\begin{array}{l} \textbf{5 parts = £60} \\ \textbf{1 part = £12} \end{array} \right) ÷5$$

Since we now know the 'value' of 1 part we can work out how much money Jon and Pat get.

Jon gets 2 parts = 2 × £12 = £24
Pat gets 3 parts = 3 × £12 = £36

> Check: £24 + £36 = £60

2 Three brothers aged 6, 9 and 15 decide to share a tin of toffees in the ratio of their ages. If the tin contains 240 toffees how many toffees does each brother get?

We need to divide 240 toffees in the ratio 6 : 9 : 15

> Whenever possible cancel down your ratio to make things simpler

$$÷3 \left(\begin{array}{l} \textbf{6 : 9 : 15} \\ \textbf{= 2 : 3 : 5} \end{array} \right) ÷3$$

Total number of parts
= 2 + 3 + 5 = 10 parts

Therefore…

$$÷10 \left(\begin{array}{l} \textbf{10 parts = 240 toffees} \\ \textbf{1 part = 24 toffees} \end{array} \right) ÷10$$

Brother aged 6 gets 2 × 24 = 48 toffees
Brother aged 9 gets 3 × 24 = 72 toffees
Brother aged 15 gets 5 × 24 = 120 toffees

> Check: 48 + 72 + 120 = 240 toffees

Increasing and Decreasing a Quantity in Direct Proportion

Example
A recipe to make 10 flapjacks requires, among other ingredients, 180g of butter. How much butter does a cook need to use if they want to make…
a) 6 flapjacks?
b) 25 flapjacks?

This is an example of a quantity (e.g. butter) that increases or decreases in direct proportion to the amount of baking needed. The more baking needed the greater the amount of butter needed and vice versa.

The easiest way is to work out the amount of butter needed to make 1 flapjack.

$$÷10 \left(\begin{array}{l} \text{10 flapjacks require 180g of butter} \\ \text{1 flapjack requires 18g of butter} \end{array} \right) ÷10$$

a) 6 flapjacks require
6 × 18g **= 108g of butter**

b) 25 flapjacks require
25 × 18g **= 450g of butter**

Estimating Answers

Answers to many calculations can be estimated by rounding off numbers within the calculations to 1 or 2 significant figures.

Examples

Estimate the answers to the following calculations:

1 $71 + 18 - 26$

$\approx 70 + 20 - 30$

$\approx$ **60 (Actual answer is 63)**

2 $\dfrac{43 \times 2.9}{61.34}$

$\approx \dfrac{40 \times 3}{60}$

$\approx \dfrac{120}{60}$

$\approx$ **2 (Actual answer is 2.03 (2 d.p.))**

3 $\dfrac{3.6 \times 10.4}{7.7 - 3.1}$

$\approx \dfrac{4 \times 10}{8 - 3}$

$\approx \dfrac{40}{5}$

$\approx$ **8 (Actual answer is 8.14 (2 d.p.))**

4 $\dfrac{413 \times 4.87}{0.189}$

$\approx \dfrac{400 \times 5}{0.2}$

$\approx \dfrac{2000}{0.2}$

$\approx$ **10 000 (Actual answer is 10 600 (3 s.f.))**

5 $\sqrt{82.35}$

$\approx \sqrt{81}$

$\approx$ **9 (81 is a square number close to 82.35)**

Checking your Answers for Accuracy

Answers to calculations can be checked for accuracy by starting with your answer and working backwards, reversing the operations.

Examples

Check the answers to the following calculations:

1 $8 \times 7 = 56 \longrightarrow \dfrac{56}{8} = \mathbf{7}\checkmark$ or $\dfrac{56}{7} = \mathbf{8}\checkmark$

2 The table below shows the amount of money collected by a small local charity from October to December, using collecting tins at three different locations. Check it for accuracy.

Month	Location 1	Location 2	Location 3	Total
Oct	28.08	16.73	18.23	63.04
Nov	32.96	21.01	18.16	72.13
Dec	26.12	19.57	16.03	61.72
Total	87.16	57.31	52.42	**196.89**

Vertical totals

$63.04 + 72.13 + 61.72 =$ **196.89**

Horizontal totals

$87.16 + 57.31 + 52.42 =$ **196.89**

The overall total is the same in each case. This is known as a cross-check.

Algebraic Expressions

Algebra is a branch of mathematics where letters and other symbols are used to represent numbers and quantities in expressions, equations, identities and formulae. Algebra follows the same rules as arithmetic.

Algebraic Expressions

An algebraic expression is a collection of connected letters, numbers and arithmetical symbols. Here are some simple expressions and their meanings.

Algebraic Expression	What it Means
$2a$	$2 \times a$ or $a + a$
ab	$a \times b$ (or $b \times a$)
$\dfrac{a}{b}$	$a \div b$
$3a - b$	$(3 \times a) - b$
c^2	$c \times c$
$4mn$	$4 \times m \times n$
x^2	$x \times x$
a^3	$a \times a \times a$
$4x^2y$	$4 \times x \times x \times y$
$(4a)^2$	$4a \times 4a$

Collecting Like Terms

Many expressions can be simplified by collecting together like terms, e.g. all the xs or all the x^2s.

Examples

1. $a + 2a$ is **3a**

2. $5x - 8x + 7x$ is **4x**

When your expression contains 'different' terms, rearrange and collect together all like terms before you simplify.

Examples

1. $6b + 3c - 4b$
$= 6b - 4b + 3c$
     └─┘
     Like terms
$= \mathbf{2b + 3c}$

2. $-4x + 3 + 7x - 8$
$= -4x + 7x + 3 - 8$
   └──┘ └──┘
   Like terms   Like terms
$= \mathbf{3x - 5}$

3. $4x + 7y - x - 3y$
$= 4x - x + 7y - 3y$
   └──┘ └──┘
   Like terms   Like terms
$= \mathbf{3x + 4y}$

4. $5pq - 7rs + 8pq + 2sr$
$= 5pq + 8pq - 7rs + 2rs$
   └──┘   └──┘
   Like terms   Like terms
   since 'pq' is the   since 'rs' is the
   same as 'qp'   same as 'sr'

$= \mathbf{13pq - 5rs}$

5. Find and simplify an expression for the perimeter, p, of the triangle below.

$2x$ $x + 5$

$2x + 3$

$p = 2x + x + 5 + 2x + 3$
$p = 2x + x + 2x + 5 + 3$
$p = 5x + 8$

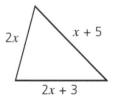

- The perimeter is all the side lengths added together.
- Collect like terms.

The Rules of Indices

Rules of Indices for Algebra

The same rules are used with algebra as we previously used with numbers (see page 14). Very simply...

1 x^1 is the same as x.

2 x^0 is equal to 1. Provided that x is not equal to 0.

3 $x^5 \times x^2$ becomes x^{5+2} and is equal to x^7
We add the powers.

4 $x^5 \div x^2$ becomes x^{5-2} and is equal to x^3
We subtract the powers.

5 x^{-1} is the same as $\frac{1}{x}$.

Examples

1 $x^2 \times x$

$= x^2 \times x^1$

$= x^{2+1}$

$= x^3$

> x is the same as x^1

> Add the powers

2 $y^3 \times 5y^4$

$= 5y^{3+4}$

$= 5y^7$

> Write the number first and add the powers.

3 $\dfrac{w^6}{w^2}$

$= w^{6-2}$

$= w^4$

> Subtract the powers to divide

4 $\dfrac{12z^{12}}{4z^4}$

$= \left(\dfrac{12}{4}\right)z^{12-4}$

$= 3z^8$

> Divide the numbers but subtract the powers

5 $2x^3 \times 4x^2$

$= (2 \times 4)x^{3+2}$

$= 8x^5$

> Multiply your numbers as normal and add the powers

6 $10r^5 \div 2r$

$= \left(\dfrac{10}{2}\right)r^{5-1}$

$= 5r^4$

> Divide your numbers as normal and subtract the powers

7 $\dfrac{5r^7 \times 4r^2}{10r^6}$

$= \dfrac{(5 \times 4)r^{7+2}}{10r^6}$

$= \left(\dfrac{20}{10}\right)r^{9-6}$

$= 2r^3$

> Do one operation at a time. Multiplication first...

> ... and then division

8 $x^4y^2 \times x^3y^6$

$= x^{4+3}\ y^{2+6}$

$= x^7y^8$

> Add the powers of x's and y's separately

Substitution

Substitution

Substitution involves substituting numbers for letters in expressions. The simplest substitution would involve only one operation (e.g. an addition or multiplication). However, when a substitution involves more than one operation, you must make them in the order shown below.

BIDMAS

| Brackets | Indices (or powers) | Divisions and Multiplications – can be done in any order | Additions and Subtractions – can be done in any order |

Since you are expected to be able to substitute positive and negative numbers into expressions, turn back to page 11 to refresh yourself on the multiplication and division of integers.

Examples

If $a = 3$, $b = 8$, $c = 20$, $d = -4$, calculate the value of...

1 $2(a + b) - c$ | Substitute in your numbers

$= 2(3 + 8) - 20$ | Work out the brackets first

$= 2 \times 11 - 20$ | Then the multiplication

$= 22 - 20$ | Then the subtraction

$= \mathbf{2}$

2 $\dfrac{c(d + 1)}{5}$ | Substitute in your numbers

$= \dfrac{20(-4 + 1)}{5}$ | Work out the brackets first

$= \dfrac{20 \times -3}{5}$ | Then the multiplication $(+ \times - = -)$

$= \dfrac{-60}{5}$ | Then the division $(- \div + = -)$

$= \mathbf{-12}$

3 $3d^2 + c$ | Substitute in your numbers

$= 3 \times (-4)^2 + 20$ | Work out the square first $(- \times - = +)$

$= 3 \times 16 + 20$ | Then the multiplication

$= 48 + 20$ | Then the addition

$= \mathbf{68}$

4 $2a^3$ | Substitute in your numbers

$= 2 \times (3)^3$ | Work out the cube first

$= 2 \times 27$ | Then the multiplication

$= \mathbf{54}$

5 $\dfrac{1}{2}d^3$ | Substitute in your numbers

$= \dfrac{1}{2} \times (-4)^3$ | Work out the cube first $(- \times - = +$ and then $+ \times - = -)$

$= \dfrac{1}{2} \times -64$ | Then the multiplication

$= \mathbf{-32}$

Multiplying Out Brackets

When we multiply out brackets, everything which is inside the brackets must be multiplied by whatever is immediately outside the brackets.

Examples

1 $4(x + 3)$
$= 4 \times x + 4 \times 3$
$= \mathbf{4x + 12}$

2 $6(3x + 2)$
$= 6 \times 3x + 6 \times 2$
$= \mathbf{18x + 12}$

3 $4(5x - 4)$
$= 4 \times 5x + 4 \times \text{-}4$
$= \mathbf{20x - 16}$

4 $5(2x + 7)$
$= 5 \times 2x + 5 \times 7$
$= \mathbf{10x + 35}$

5 $x(x + 3) - 7$
$= x \times x + x \times 3 - 7$
$= \mathbf{x^2 + 3x - 7}$

6 $2(4x + 3) + 5(x - 2)$
$= 8x + 6 + 5x - 10$
$= 8x + 5x + 6 - 10$
$\underbrace{\qquad}_{\text{Like terms}} \underbrace{\qquad}_{\text{Like terms}}$
$= \mathbf{13x - 4}$

> If your expression includes two brackets you may end up with like terms, which you need to collect together and simplify

7 $x(5 - x) + 4x(2x^2 + 3x)$
$= 5x - x^2 + 8x^3 + 12x^2$
$= 8x^3 - x^2 + 12x^2 + 5x$
$\underbrace{\qquad}_{\text{Like terms}}$
$= \mathbf{8x^3 + 11x^2 + 5x}$

8 $(x + 2)(x + 3)$
$= x(x + 3) + 2(x + 3)$
$= x^2 + 3x + 2x + 6$
$\underbrace{\qquad}_{\text{Like terms}}$
$= \mathbf{x^2 + 5x + 6}$

> When you multiply out two brackets make sure that each term in the second bracket is multiplied by each term in the first bracket.

9 $(3x - 2)^2$
$= (3x - 2)(3x - 2)$
$= 3x(3x - 2) - 2(3x - 2)$
$= 9x^2 - 6x - 6x + 4$
$\underbrace{\qquad}_{\text{Like terms}}$
$= \mathbf{9x^2 - 12x + 4}$

Factorisation

Factorisation is the reverse process to multiplying out brackets. An expression is rewritten with brackets by taking out the highest factor common to all the terms in the expression.

Examples

1 $4x + 6 = \mathbf{2(2x + 3)}$
2 is the highest common factor of both 4 and 6.

2 $4x - 12y = \mathbf{4(x - 3y)}$
as **4** is the highest factor common to both 4 and 12.

3 $3x^2 + 8x = \mathbf{x(3x + 8)}$
as $\boldsymbol{x}$ is the highest factor common to both x^2 and x.

4 $6x^2 + 8x = \mathbf{2x(3x + 4)}$
as **2** is the highest common factor of both 6 and 8 and $\boldsymbol{x}$ is the highest common factor of both x^2 and x.

Linear Equations

Linear Equations with the Unknown on One Side of the Equation

Equations such as…

$$4x = 12$$
$$x + 3 = 7$$
$$2(x + 5) = 14$$

… are all examples of linear equations since the highest power they contain is x^1 (i.e. x).

Each of these linear equations can be solved to find the 'unknown' value of x by doing the same thing to both sides of the equation. The simplest linear equation would involve one operation to solve it. Most, however, require at least two operations.

Examples

1 $6x = 18$

$$\frac{\cancel{6}x}{\cancel{6}} = \frac{18}{6}$$

$$x = 3$$

> Divide both sides of the equation by **6** to leave just x on the left-hand side.

2 $3x - 5 = 19$

$$3x - \cancel{5} + \cancel{5} = 19 + 5$$

$$\frac{\cancel{3}x}{\cancel{3}} = \frac{24}{3}$$

$$x = 8$$

> Add **5** to both sides of the equation to remove the **-5** from the left-hand side.

> Divide both sides of the equation by **3** to leave just x on the left-hand side.

3 $18 = 4(x + 3)$

$$18 = 4x + 12$$

$$18 - 12 = 4x + \cancel{12} - \cancel{12}$$

$$\frac{-6}{4} = \frac{\cancel{4}x}{\cancel{4}}$$

$$\mathbf{1.5} = x$$

$$\text{or } x = \mathbf{1.5}$$

> Multiply out the bracket on the right-hand side.

> Subtract **12** from both sides of the equation to remove the **+12** on the right-hand side.

> Divide both sides of the equation by **4** to leave just x on the right-hand side.

4 $\dfrac{x + 3}{4} = 5$

$$\frac{x + 3}{\cancel{4}} \times \cancel{4} = 5 \times 4$$

$$x + 3 = 20$$

$$x + \cancel{3} - \cancel{3} = 20 - 3$$

$$x = \mathbf{17}$$

> Multiply both sides of the equation by **4** to remove the **4** from the left-hand side.

> Subtract **3** from both sides of the equation to leave just x on the left-hand side.

5 $5(x + 6) = 20$

$$5x + 30 = 20$$

$$5x + \cancel{30} - \cancel{30} = 20 - 30$$

$$\frac{\cancel{5}x}{\cancel{5}} = \frac{-10}{5}$$

$$x = -2$$

> Multiply out the bracket on the left-hand side.

> Subtract **30** from both sides of the equation to remove the **+30** on the left-hand side.

> Divide both sides of the equation by **5** to leave just x on the left-hand side.

Linear Equations

Linear Equations with the Unknown on Both Sides of the Equation

The following examples have the 'unknown', e.g. x, appearing on both sides of the equation. Once again they are solved by collecting all the x's on one side and all the numbers on the other side.

It does not really matter on which side of the equal sign you collect all the x's, it is your choice. In the examples below, they are collected on the side that has the most positive x's to start with. This ensures that you end up with a value for x rather than $-x$.

Examples

 1

$$8x - 7 = 5x + 2$$

$$8x - 5x - 7 = 5x - 5x + 2$$

$$3x - 7 + 7 = 2 + 7$$

$$\frac{3x}{3} = \frac{9}{3}$$

$$x = 3$$

> Subtract **5x** from both sides of the equation to leave all the x's on the left-hand side.

> Add **7** to both sides of the equation to remove the **−7** on the left-hand side.

> Divide both sides of the equation by **3** to leave just x on the left-hand side.

2

$$4(3x - 2) = 14x + 4$$

$$12x - 8 = 14x + 4$$

$$12x - 12x - 8 = 14x - 12x + 4$$

$$-8 - 4 = 2x + 4 - 4$$

$$\frac{-12}{2} = \frac{2x}{2}$$

$$-6 = x$$

$$\text{or } x = -6$$

> Multiply out the bracket on the left-hand side.

> Subtract **12x** from both sides of the equation to leave all the xs on the right-hand side.

> Subtract **4** from both sides of the equation to remove the **4** on the right-hand side.

> Divide both sides of the equation by **2** to leave just x on the right-hand side.

Problem Solving Using Linear Equations

Problem solving using linear equations involves being given information, forming a linear equation from the information given and then solving the equation.

Example

The four angles of a quadrilateral are: a, $a + 20°$, $a + 40°$ and $a + 60°$. Calculate the size of each angle.

We know that the angles of a quadrilateral add up to **360°**.
Therefore, it follows that:

$$a + (a + 20) + (a + 40) + (a + 60) = 360$$
$$4a + 120 = 360$$
$$4a = 240$$
$$a = 60°$$

> Subtract 120 from both sides
> Divide both sides by 4

$a = 60°$, $a + 20° = 80°$, $a + 40° = 100°$, $a + 60° = 120°$.

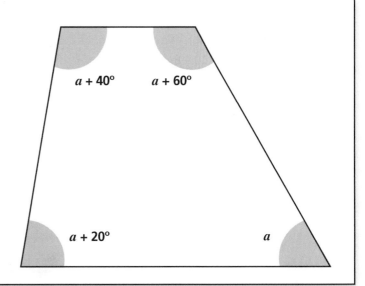

Formulae

Changing the Subject of a Formula

Formulae show the relationship between two or more changeable quantities (variables). They can be written in words, but most often symbols are used instead.

For example, the area of a circle is given by the following formula, which describes the relationship between the area of a circle and its radius:

$$A = \pi r^2$$

Formulae can be rearranged to make a different letter the 'subject', e.g. **a = b + c** has **a** as the subject since it is on one side by itself. If we wanted to make **b** or **c** the subject then we would need to rearrange the formula by moving terms from one side of the equals sign to the other.

Examples

1 Make **b** the subject of the following formula.

$a = b + c$

$a - c = b + \cancel{c} - \cancel{c}$

$\boldsymbol{b = a - c}$

> Subtract **c** from both sides of the formula. This will remove the +**c** on the right-hand side to leave **b** on its own.

> Rewrite the formula with **b** on the left-hand side.

2 Make **y** the subject of the following equation.

$x + y = 7$

$\cancel{x} - \cancel{x} + y = 7 - x$

$\boldsymbol{y = 7 - x}$

or $\boldsymbol{y = \text{-}x + 7}$

> Subtract **x** from both sides of the formula to remove the **x** on the left-hand side.

3 Make **x** the subject of the following equation.

$4(3x + 2y) = 10$

$4 \times 3x + 4 \times 2y = 10$

$12x + 8y = 10$

$12x + \cancel{8y} - \cancel{8y} = 10 - 8y$

$\dfrac{\cancel{12}x}{\cancel{12}} = \dfrac{10 - 8y}{12}$

$x = \dfrac{\mathbf{10 - 8y}}{\mathbf{12}}$

> Multiply out the bracket on the left-hand side.

> Subtract **8y** from both sides of the formula to remove the **+8y** on the left-hand side.

> Divide both sides of the formula by **12** to leave just **x** on the left-hand side.

4 Make **r** the subject of the following formula.

$A = \pi r^2$

$\dfrac{A}{\pi} = \dfrac{\cancel{\pi} r^2}{\cancel{\pi}}$

$\sqrt{\dfrac{A}{\pi}} = \cancel{\sqrt{r^2}}$

$\boldsymbol{r = \sqrt{\dfrac{A}{\pi}}}$

> Divide both sides of the formula by π to remove the π on the right-hand side

> Take the square root of both sides of the formula to remove the 'square' and leave just **r** on the right-hand side.

> Rewrite the formula with **r** on the left-hand side.

Formulae

Using Formulae

Examples

1 A company hires a temporary member of staff. If the temp works 32 hours at a rate of £6 per hour, calculate the cost of hiring using the following formula:

> **wage earned = hours worked × rate per hour**

All we have to do is substitute values into our formula.

$$\text{wage earned} = \text{hours worked} \times \text{rate per hour}$$
$$= 32 \text{ hours} \times £6$$
$$= \textbf{£192}$$

2 The following formula converts a temperature reading from degrees Celsius (°C) into degrees Fahrenheit (°F):

> **$F = \frac{9}{5}C + 32$**

What is the temperature in degrees Fahrenheit if the temperature in degrees Celsius is 25°C?

$$F = \frac{9}{5}C + 32$$
$$F = \frac{9}{5} \times 25 + 32$$
$$F = 45 + 32$$
$$\textbf{F = 77°F}$$

*We now substitute into our formula a value for **C**, which is 25°C, to work out **F**.*

3 The area of a triangle is given by the formula:

> **$A = \frac{b \times h}{2}$**

where **b** is length of base and **h** is height of triangle.

Calculate the area of a triangle if the length of its base is 10cm and its height is 6cm.

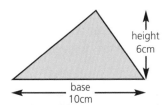

height
6cm

base
10cm

$$A = \frac{b \times h}{2}$$
$$= \frac{10 \times 6}{2}$$
$$= \frac{60}{2}$$
$$= \textbf{30cm}^2$$

*All we need to do is substitute values for **b** and **h** into our formula.*

Deriving Formulae

Deriving formulae means to make a formula from given information. You may then need to use this formula to work out an unknown quantity.

Example

Derive a formulae for the perimeter of a rectangle in terms of its area, **A**, and width, **w**, only. Use it to work out the perimeter if area = 40cm² and width = 4cm

$$l = \frac{A}{w}$$

Perimeter = $2l + 2w$

Length (l)

width (w)

Perimeter $= 2l + 2w$
$$= 2\frac{A}{w} + 2w$$
$$= \frac{2A}{w} + 2w$$
$$= \frac{2 \times 40}{4} + 2 \times 4$$
$$= \frac{80}{4} + 8$$
$$= 20 + 8$$
$$= \textbf{28cm}$$

*Firstly, we need to substitute $\frac{A}{w}$ for **l** in our formula for perimeter, to give us the formula in terms of area and width only. All we do then is substitute in values for **A** and **w** to find the perimeter.*

Trial & Improvement

Solving Equations by Trial and Improvement

This method can be used to find a solution to any equation. As the name suggests we trial a possible solution by substituting its value into the equation.

The process is then repeated using a different possible solution and so on. The idea is that each subsequent trial is an improvement on the previous trial.

Examples

1 The equation $x^2 - 2x = 18$ has a solution somewhere between $x = 5$ and $x = 6$. By trial and improvement, calculate a solution to the equation to 1 decimal place.

Since we are told that there is a solution between $x = 5$ and $x = 6$ we will substitute these values into our equation to see what $x^2 - 2x$ gives us. Remember we want its value to be equal to $x^2 - 2x = 18$.

x	$x^2 - 2x$	Comment
5	$5^2 - (2 \times 5)$ $= 25 - 10$ $= 15$	Less than 18
6	$6^2 - (2 \times 6)$ $= 36 - 12$ $= 24$	More than 18
Try 5.5	$5.5^2 - (2 \times 5.5)$ $= 30.25 - 11$ $= 19.25$	More than 18
Try 5.4	$5.4^2 - (2 \times 5.4)$ $= 29.16 - 10.8$ $= 18.36$	More than 18
Try 5.3	$5.3^2 - (2 \times 5.3)$ $= 28.09 - 10.6$ $= 17.49$	Less than 18
Try 5.35	$3.35^2 - (2 \times 5.35)$ $= 28.6225 - 10.7$ $= 17.9225$	Just less than 18

So $x = 5.4$ (to 1 d.p.) since the last trial of 5.35 is less than 18.

If the last trial had been more than 18 then the solution would have been $x = 5.3$ (to 1 d.p.). It is important to try the middle value (**5.35**) just to be sure.

2 Using trial and improvement, calculate the solution to the equation $x^3 + x = 37$ to 2 decimal places.

With this equation you are given no hints to the value of x, so you must make a 'guestimate' to start.

x	$x^3 + x$	Comment
Try 3	$3^3 + 3$ $= 27 + 3$ $= 30$	Less than 37
Try 4	$4^3 + 4$ $= 64 + 4$ $= 68$	More than 37
Try 3.5	$3.5^3 + 3.5$ $= 42.875 + 3.5$ $= 46.375$	More than 37
Try 3.4	$3.4^3 + 3.4$ $= 39.304 + 3.4$ $= 42.704$	More than 37
Try 3.3	$3.3^3 + 3.3$ $= 35.937 + 3.3$ $= 39.237$	More than 37
Try 3.2	$3.2^3 + 3.2$ $= 32.768 + 3.2$ $= 35.968$	Less than 37
Try 3.25	$3.25^3 + 3.25$ $= 34.328125 + 3.25$ $= 37.578125$	More than 37
Try 3.24	$3.24^3 + 3.24$ $= 34.012224 + 3.24$ $= 37.252224$	More than 37
Try 3.23	$3.23^3 + 3.23$ $= 33.698267 + 3.23$ $= 36.928267$	Less than 37
Try 3.235	$3.235^3 + 3.235$ $= 33.85500288 + 3.235$ $= 37.090$	Just more than 37

So $x = 3.23$ (to 2 d.p.) since the final trial was slightly more than 37. If the final trial had been less than 37 then the solution would be $x = 3.24$ (to 2 d.p.). Remember to try the middle value (3.235).

Sequences

Number Patterns and Sequences

A number pattern or sequence is a series of numbers which follow a rule. Each number in a sequence is called a **term**, where the first number in the sequence is called the **1st term** and so on.

| 1st term | 2nd term | 3rd term | 4th term | | The next two terms |

2,   **6,**   **10,**   **14,...**

+4   +4   +4

The rule is that each term is **4 more** than the previous term. These terms have a common difference of +4

...18,   22, ...

+4

20,   17,   14,   11,...

-3   -3   -3

The rule is that each term is **3 less** than the previous term. These terms have a common difference of -3

... 8,   5, ...

-3

1,   3,   9,   27,...

×3   ×3   ×3

The rule is that each term is **3 times** the previous term. These terms don't have a common difference between them

...81,   243,...

×3

A sequence can also be a series of diagrams.

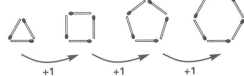

+2   +2   +2

Each diagram (term) has **2 more** boxes in it than the previous diagram. These diagrams have a common difference of +2

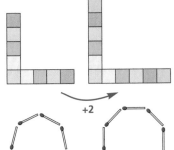

+2

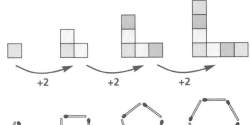

+1   +1   +1

Each diagram (term) has **1 more** match in it than the previous diagram. These diagrams have a common difference of +1

+1

Examples

1 Squared integers

1,   **4,**   **9,**   **16, ...**

$(1^2 = 1)$ $(2^2 = 4)$ $(3^2 = 9)$ $(4^2 = 16)$

2 Triangular numbers

1,   **3,**   **6,**   **10,...**

+2   +3   +4

3 Powers of 2

1,   **2,**   **4,**   **8, ...**

$(2^0 = 1)$ $(2^1 = 2)$ $(2^2 = 4)$ $(2^3 = 8)$

4 Powers of 10

1,   **10,**   **100,**   **1000,...**

$(10^0 = 1)$ $(10^1 = 10)$ $(10^2 = 100)$ $(10^3 = 1000)$

Sequences

The nth Term of a Sequence

The nth term is a formula that enables us to generate any term within a particular sequence.

Example

Let our sequence of numbers have an **nth term = $2n + 2$**, where **n** is the position of the term, i.e. the first term has **$n = 1$**, the second term has **$n = 2$** and so on. This formula now enables us to generate any term simply by substituting our value for n into the formula.

nth term $= 2n + 2$
1st term $= 2 \times 1 + 2 = 4$
2nd term $= 2 \times 2 + 2 = 6$
3rd term $= 2 \times 3 + 2 = 8$
4th term $= 2 \times 4 + 2 = 10$
100th term $= 2 \times 100 + 2 = 202$

So, our sequence of numbers would look like…
4, 6, 8, 10, …

Finding the nth term of an Arithmetic Sequence

A sequence where there is a common difference between the terms can be described by a linear algebraic expression. The general formula for the nth term of these sequences is as follows:

nth term = $an + b$

where **a** is the common difference between the terms and **b** is a constant.

The first thing you do is determine the value of **a**. To then find **b** substitute the value for the 1st term, **$n = 1$** and **a** into the formula.

Examples

① **5,   7,   9,   11,…**
$+2$ $+2$ $+2$

These terms have a common difference of **+2** and so **$a = 2$**. If we take the 1st term then **$n = 1$** and it has a value of **5**. We then substitute these values into the formula…

nth term $= an + b$
$5 = 2 \times 1 + b$

… to give us $b = 5 - 2 = 3$

… Therefore **nth term = $2n + 3$**

… To check **2nd term $= 2 \times 2 + 3 = 4 + 3 = 7$** ✓
        3rd term $= 2 \times 3 + 3 = 6 + 3 = 9$ ✓

② **20,   17,   14,   11,…**
-3 -3 -3

These terms have a common difference of **-3** and so **$a = -3$**. If we take the 1st term then **$n = 1$** and it has a value of **20**. We then substitute these values into the formula…

nth term $= an + b$
$20 = -3 \times 1 + b$

… to give us $b = 20 + 3 = 23$

… Therefore **nth term = $-3n + 23$**

… To check **2nd term $= -3 \times 2 + 23 = -6 + 23 = 17$** ✓
        3rd term $= -3 \times 3 + 23 = -9 + 23 = 14$ ✓

Plotting Points

xy

All points are plotted on graph or squared paper. Usually your graph or squared paper is divided into four sections called **quadrants** by two lines known as the **x-axis**, which is a horizontal line, and the **y-axis**, which is a vertical line. The point where the two axes cross is called the **origin** (0,0).

The position of any plotted point is given by its **coordinates**. All coordinates are written as two numbers in a bracket separated by a comma, e.g. (3,4) (5,-2), where…

- the first number represents the **x** coordinate, which is read going across horizontally to the right (positive) or left (negative).
- the second number represents the **y** coordinate which is read vertically going up (positive) or down (negative).

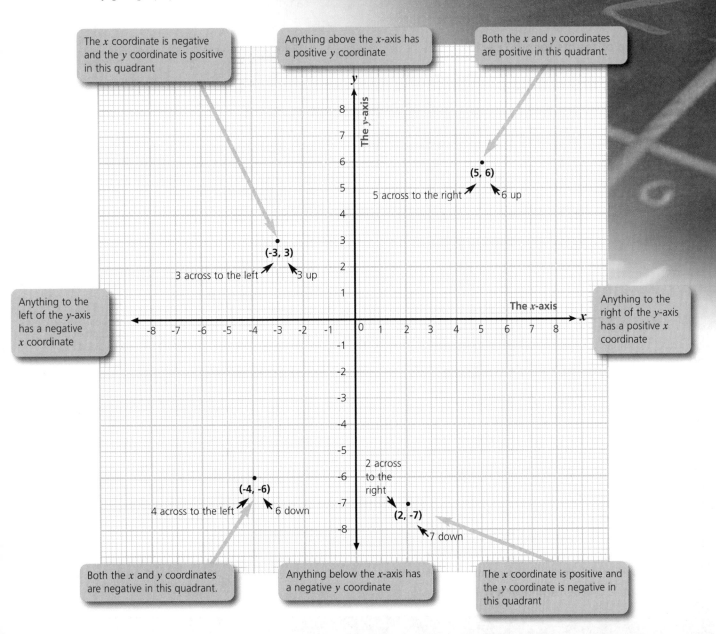

The x coordinate is negative and the y coordinate is positive in this quadrant

Anything above the x-axis has a positive y coordinate

Both the x and y coordinates are positive in this quadrant.

(5, 6)

5 across to the right   6 up

(-3, 3)

3 across to the left   3 up

Anything to the left of the y-axis has a negative x coordinate

The x-axis

Anything to the right of the y-axis has a positive x coordinate

(-4, -6)

4 across to the left   6 down

2 across to the right

(2, -7)

7 down

Both the x and y coordinates are negative in this quadrant.

Anything below the x-axis has a negative y coordinate

The x coordinate is positive and the y coordinate is negative in this quadrant

Straight Line Graphs

Graphs of Linear Functions

A linear function, e.g. $y = x$, $y = 2x - 1$, $y = 0.5x + 1$, is a function that may be written in the form $ax + b$, where a and b are constants. This will always give you a straight line graph when drawn.

To draw the graph of a linear function you only need to plot three points.

Examples

1 Draw the graph of $y = 2x - 1$ for values of between **-2** and **2** (this may be written **-2 ⩽ x ⩽ 2**).

Firstly, we need to pick 3 values of x, within the range, so that we can work out their y values. The two extreme values of x and one in the middle will do. Draw a table of results as follows:

Table of results for $y = 2x - 1$

x	-2	0	2
$2x$	(2 × -2 =) -4	(2 × 0 =) 0	(2 × 2 =) 4
-1	-1	-1	-1
$y = 2x - 1$	(-4 - 1 =) **-5**	(0 - 1 =) **-1**	(4 - 1 =) **3**

We now have the coordinates of 3 points – (-2,-5), (0,-1) and (2,3) – and can plot our graph.

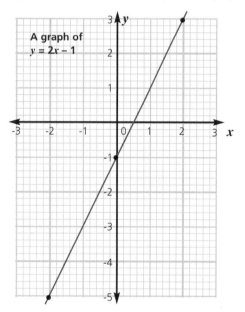

A graph of
$y = 2x - 1$

Remember your straight line must pass through all 3 points! If it doesn't then one of your points is wrong. You can either check your table again or better still work out the coordinates of another point, e.g. when $x = $ **-1** or $x = $ **1**.

2 Draw the graph of **2y + x = 4** for values of between **-2** and **2**.

The first thing we have to do is rearrange the function to make **y** the subject. When we have done that we can draw a table of results.

$$2y + x = 4$$
$$2y + x - x = -x + 4 \quad \text{(Subtract } x \text{ from both sides)}$$
$$\frac{2y}{2} = \frac{-x}{2} + \frac{4}{2} \quad \text{(Divide both sides by 2)}$$
$$y = -0.5x + 2$$

Table of results for $y = -0.5x + 2$

x	-2	0	2
$-0.5x$	(-0.5 × -2 =) 1	(-0.5 × 0 =) 0	(-0.5 × 2 =) -1
+ 2	+2	+2	+2
$y = -0.5x + 2$	(1 + 2 =) **3**	(0 + 2 =) **2**	(-1 + 2 =) **1**

We now have the coordinates of 3 points – (-2,3), (0,2) and (2,1) – and can plot our graph.

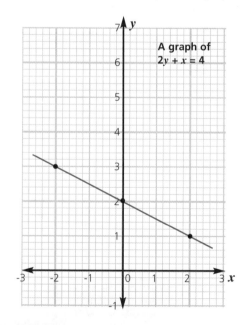

A graph of
$2y + x = 4$

Straight Line Graphs

Graphs of Linear Functions (Cont.)

Examples

3 Draw the graph of **y − 2x = 1** for values of **x** between -2 and 2.

The first thing we have to do is rearrange the function to make **y** the subject. When we have done that we can draw a table of results.

$$y - 2x = 1$$
$$y - 2\!\!\!/x + 2\!\!\!/x = 1 + 2x$$
$$y = 2x + 1$$

Add 2x to both sides to leave just y on the left-hand side

Table of results for y = 2x + 1

x	-2	0	2
2x	(2 × -2 =) -4	(2 × 0 =) 0	(2 × 2 =) 4
+1	+1	+1	+1
y = 2x + 1	(-4 + 1 =) -3	(0 + 1 =) 1	(4 + 1 =) 5

We now have the coordinates of 3 points – (-2,-3), (0,1) and (2,5) and can plot our graph.

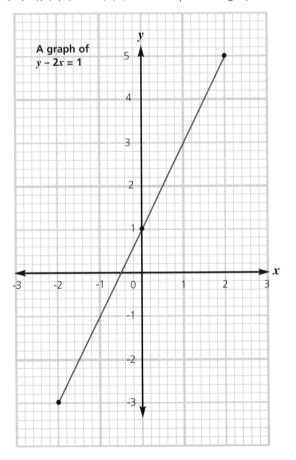

A graph of
y − 2x = 1

4 Draw the graph of **x + y = 3** for values of **x** between **-2** and **2**.

$$x + y = 3$$
$$\not{x} + \not{x} + y = 3 - x$$
$$y = \text{-}x + 3$$

Subtract x from both sides to leave just y on the left-hand side

Table of results for y = -x + 3

x	-2	0	2
-x	(− -2 =) 2	(-0 =) 0	(-2 =) -2
+ 3	+ 3	+ 3	+ 3
y = -x+3	(2 + 3 =) 5	(0 + 3 =) 3	(-2 + 3 =) 1

We now have the coordinates of 3 points – (-2,5), (0,3) and (2,1) and can plot our graph.

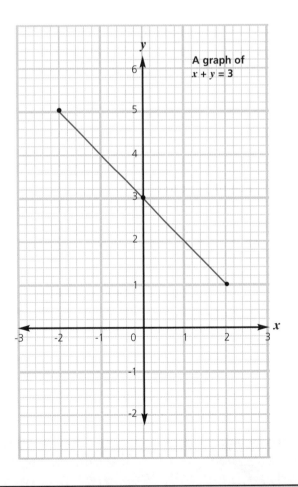

A graph of
x + y = 3

Straight Line Graphs

Types of Straight Line Graph

Examples

1 Graph of x = 'A Number'

Examples are $x = 4$, $x = -3$, $x = 0$. The graphs of these equations are all vertical lines, i.e. they all go straight up and down.

For the graph x = 'A Number' the x coordinates of all points on the line are always the same and are equal to the 'number'. However, all the points will have different y coordinates.

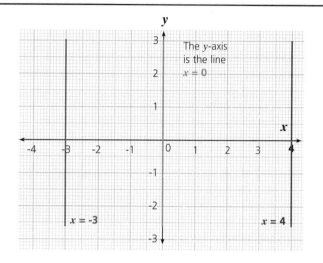

2 Graph of y = 'A Number'

Examples are $y = 3$, $y = -2$, $y = 0$. The graphs of these equations are all horizontal lines, i.e. they all go straight across.

For the graph y = 'A Number' the y coordinates of all points on the line are always the same and are equal to the 'number'. This time, however, all the points will have different x coordinates.

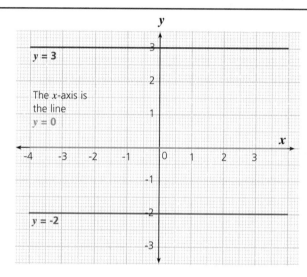

3 Graph of $y = x$ and $y = -x$

The graphs of these equations are both diagonal lines but in opposite directions. Both lines always pass through the origin (0,0) and have a gradient of 1 and -1 respectively.

For the graph $y = x$, the x and y coordinates of a particular point on the line will be the same numerically and of the same sign (both + or both -).

For the graph $y = -x$, the x and y coordinates of a particular point on the line will be the same numerically, but of opposite signs.

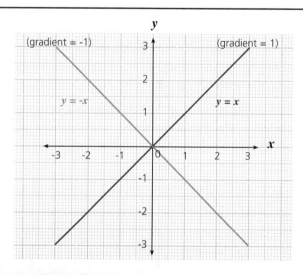

Straight Line Graphs

$$xy$$

Finding the Equation of a Straight Line

In order to find the equation of a straight line graph, all you have to do is find the gradient, **m**, and the intercept, **c**. Once you've got values for **m** and **c** you can substitute them into the following general equation to give the equation of the line:

$$y = mx + c$$

To find the gradient of a line pick two suitable points on your line and then complete a right-angled triangle as shown in the examples below. The gradient is given by the formula:

$$\textbf{Gradient} = \frac{\textbf{y change}}{\textbf{x change}}$$ For a positive gradient (see example 1)

$$\textbf{Gradient} = -\frac{\textbf{y change}}{\textbf{x change}}$$ For a negative gradient (see example 2)

Remember your measurement for the y change and the x change must be taken using the scales on the axes. You cannot measure them with a ruler.

Examples

1 For this line, gradient, **m**, is positive and so…

$$m = \frac{y\ \textbf{change}}{x\ \textbf{change}} = \frac{(6-2)}{(4-2)} = \frac{4}{2} = 2$$

Intercept, **c = -2**.

The general equation is **y = mx + c** and so the equation of this line is **y = 2x − 2**.

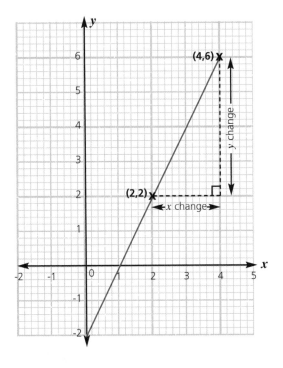

2 For this line, gradient, **m**, is negative and so…

$$m = -\frac{y\ \textbf{change}}{x\ \textbf{change}} = -\frac{(4-1)}{(4-1)} = -\frac{3}{3} = -1$$

Intercept, **c = +5**.

The general equation is **y = mx + c** and so the equation of this line is **y = -1x + 5** or **y = -x + 5**.

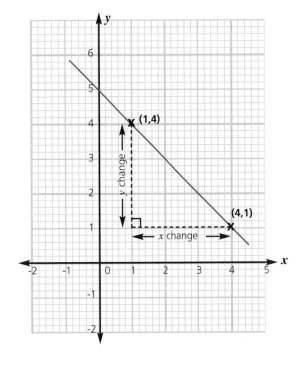

Linear Inequalities

Four Kinds of Inequality

1 **>** **which means 'Greater than'**

e.g. if *x* > 4 then *x* can have any value 'greater than' 4 but it can't have a value equal to 4.

This inequality can be shown using a number line. An open ○ circle means that *x* = 4 is not included in the inequality.

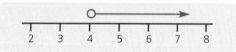

2 **≥** **which means 'Greater than or Equal to'**

e.g. if *x* ≥ 4 then *x* can have any value 'greater than' 4 and its value can also be 'equal to' 4.

This inequality can be shown using a number line. A closed ● circle means that *x* = 4 is included in the inequality.

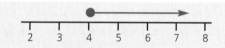

3 **<** **which means 'Less than'**

e.g. if *x* < 1 then *x* can have any value 'less than' 1 but it can't have a value equal to 1.

This inequality can be shown using a number line. An open ○ circle means that *x* = 1 is not included in the inequality.

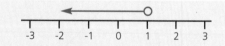

4 **≤** **which means 'Less than or Equal to'**

e.g. if *x* ≤ 1 then *x* can have any value 'less than' 1 and its value can also be 'equal to' 1.

This inequality can be shown using a number line. A closed ● circle means that *x* = 1 is included in the inequality.

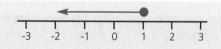

Number lines can also be used to show a combination of inequalities, for example…

1 **-2 ≤ *x* < 5.**

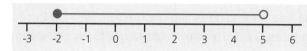

2 **1 < *x* ≤ 4**

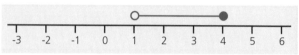

Solving Linear Inequalities

Solving linear inequalities is just like solving linear equations except we have an inequality sign instead of the equal sign.

Examples

1
$$x + 2 < 8$$
$$x + \cancel{2} - \cancel{2} < 8 - 2$$
$$\mathbf{x < 6}$$

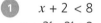

2
$$3x - 3 \geq x + 7$$
$$3x - x - 3 \geq \cancel{x} - \cancel{x} + 7$$
$$2x - \cancel{3} + \cancel{3} \geq 7 + 3$$
$$\frac{\cancel{2}x}{\cancel{2}} \geq \frac{10}{2}$$
$$\mathbf{x \geq 5}$$

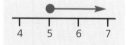

However, if you multiply or divide an inequality by a negative number then you must always reverse the direction of the inequality sign.

Examples

1
$$-2x > 6$$
$$\frac{-\cancel{2}x}{\cancel{-2}} < \frac{6}{-2}$$
$$\mathbf{x < -3}$$

> Divide both sides by -2… inequality sign reverses direction (i.e. > becomes <)

2
$$\frac{-x}{4} \leq 1.5$$
$$\frac{\cancel{/}x}{\cancel{4}} \times -\cancel{4} \geq 1.5 \times -4$$
$$\mathbf{x \geq -6}$$

> Multiply both sides by -4… inequality sign reverses direction (i.e. ≤ becomes ≥)

Graphs of Quadratic Functions

Drawing Graphs of Quadratic Functions

A quadratic function is one that can be put in the form $y = ax^2 + bx + c$. Examples would include $y = x^2$, $y = x^2 - 5$, $y = x^2 - 2x$, $y = x^2 + 4$. These functions always produce a curved graph such as the ones below. To draw a curved graph we need to plot a **full range of points** as this increases the accuracy of our curve (compare this with straight line graphs).

Examples

1 Draw the graph of $y = x^2$ for values of x between **-3** and **3** (**-3** $\leqslant x \leqslant$ **3**).

Table of results for $y = x^2$

x	-3	-2	-1	0	1	2	3
$y = x^2$	$(-3)^2=$ 9	$(-2)^2=$ 4	$(-1)^2=$ 1	$(0)^2=$ 0	$(1)^2=$ 1	$(2)^2=$ 4	$(3)^2=$ 9

We now have the coordinates of 7 points, so we can draw our graph.

Remember your curve must be smooth and it must pass through all of the points plotted.

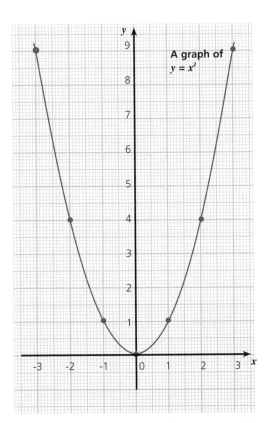

A graph of $y = x^2$

2 Draw the graph of $y = x^2 - 2x - 2$ for values of x between **-2** and **4** (**-2** $\leqslant x \leqslant$ **4**).

Table of results for $y = x^2 - 2x - 2$

x	-2	-1	0	1	2	3	4
x^2	$(-2)^2=$ 4	$(-1)^2=$ 1	$(0)^2=$ 0	$(1)^2=$ 1	$(2)^2=$ 4	$(3)^2=$ 9	$(4)^2=$ 16
$-2x$	-2×-2= +4	-2×-1= +2	-2×0= 0	-2×1= -2	-2×2= -4	-2×3= -6	-2×4= -8
-2	-2	-2	-2	-2	-2	-2	-2
$y=x^2-2x-2$	6	1	-2	-3	-2	1	6

Again we have the coordinates of 7 points, so we can draw our graph.

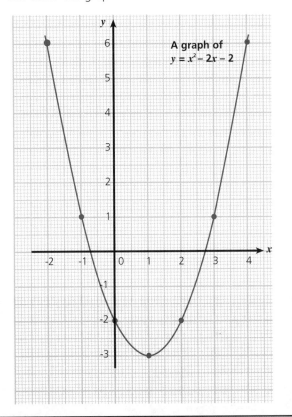

A graph of $y = x^2 - 2x - 2$

Graphs of Quadratic Functions

Solving Equations Graphically

Graphs of quadratic functions may be used to find approximate solutions to quadratic equations.

Examples

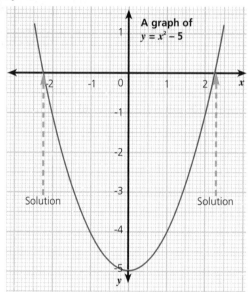

A graph of $y = x^2 - 5$

The graph of $y = x^2 - 5$ shown above may be used to solve the equation $x^2 - 5 = 0$.

On the graph, $x^2 - 5 = 0$ at the points where $y = 0$. This is where the curve crosses the x-axis.

There are two solutions, one negative and one positive.

They are approximately $x = -2.2$ and $x = 2.2$

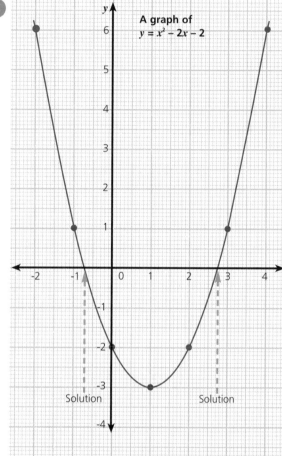

A graph of $y = x^2 - 2x - 2$

The graph of $y = x^2 - 2x - 2$ shown on the right may be used to solve the equation $x^2 - 2x - 2 = 0$.

On the graph, $x^2 - 2x - 2 = 0$ at the points where $y = 0$. This is where the curve crosses the x-axis.

There are two solutions, one negative and one positive.

They are approximately $x = -0.7$ and $x = 2.7$

Real-life Graphs

Graphs that Describe Real-life Situations

Examples

The table below shows the prices charged by a car hire firm.

Fixed Charge £20
Cost per day £10

a) What is the relationship between cost of hire and number of days hire?

b) Draw a table to show cost of hire up to 7 days and then a graph to show the relationship between cost of hire and number of days hire.

a) Using the information given, the relationship is…
Cost of hire
= Fixed charge + (Cost per day × Number of days)
If we now substitute our fixed charge and cost per day into the relationship…
Cost of hire (£) = 20 + (10 × Number of days hire)

b) We can now draw a table to show the cost of hire for up to 7 days…

Number of days hire	Cost of hire (£) = 20 + (10 x Number of days hire)
1	20 + (10 × 1) = **30**
2	20 + (10 × 2) = **40**
3	20 + (10 × 3) = **50**
4	20 + (10 × 4) = **60**
5	20 + (10 × 5) = **70**
6	20 + (10 × 6) = **80**
7	20 + (10 × 7) = **90**

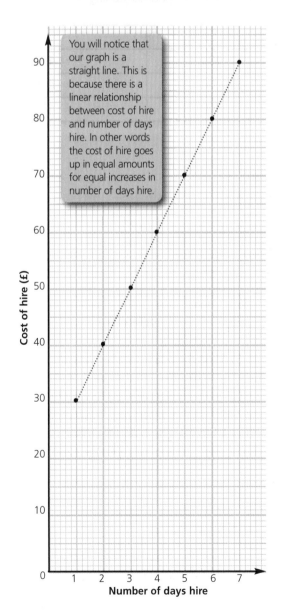

You will notice that our graph is a straight line. This is because there is a linear relationship between cost of hire and number of days hire. In other words the cost of hire goes up in equal amounts for equal increases in number of days hire.

Real-life Graphs

Conversion Graphs

Conversion graphs are used to convert values of one unit into another, e.g. pounds sterling (£) into dollars ($) or any other currency, miles into kilometres, and so on.

Examples

Draw a conversion graph for pounds sterling and dollars up to £300 if £1 = $1.60. From your graph convert…

a) £170 into dollars

b) $400 into pounds sterling.

Before we can draw our graph we need a table of values for pounds sterling and dollars.

Pounds Sterling (£)	Dollars ($)
100	(100 x 1.6 =) **160**
200	(200 x 1.6 =) **320**
300	(300 x 1.6 =) **480**

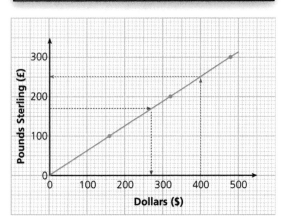

a) Go to £170 on the pounds sterling axis, draw a dotted line across (➤) to the graph and then down (▼) to the dollars axis. **£170 = $270**.

b) Go to $400 on the dollars axis, draw a dotted line up (▲) to the graph and then across (◄) to the pounds sterling axis. **$400 = £250**.

More Graphs that Describe Real-life Situations

Here are 6 examples (there are numerous others) where a graph can be used to show a real-life situation.

All of these graphs require common sense in their interpretation as each one is very different.

Examples

1 Temperature at different times in the day

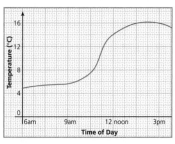

2 Weight of a man as he gets older

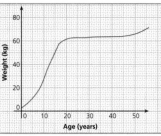

3 Value of a car as it gets older

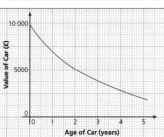

4 Pulse rate of a runner after the race is over

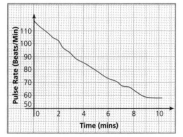

5 Height of a girl as she gets older

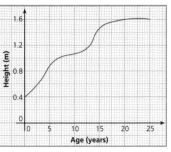

6 Temperature of a thermostatically controlled room over a period of time

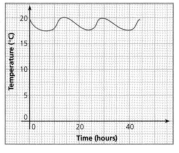

Real-life Graphs

Distance–time Graphs

Distance–time graphs are also known as travel graphs, where distance is always plotted on the vertical (**y**) axis and time is always plotted on the horizontal (**x**) axis. For a distance–time graph the slope or gradient is always equal to the speed. If there is no slope, there is no movement, i.e. speed = 0.

Example

A boy sets off from home riding his bike to go to a friend's house. A distance–time graph of his journey is shown below. Describe his movement between:

a) O and A

b) A and B

c) B and C

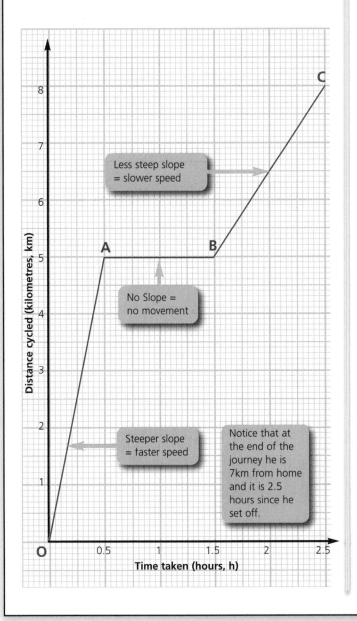

Labels on graph:
- Less steep slope = slower speed
- No Slope = no movement
- Steeper slope = faster speed
- Notice that at the end of the journey he is 7km from home and it is 2.5 hours since he set off.

y-axis: Distance cycled (kilometres, km)
x-axis: Time taken (hours, h)

a) Between O and A the boy is cycling with constant speed given by the slope or gradient.

$$\text{Speed} = \frac{\text{Distance}}{\text{Time}}$$

$$= \frac{\text{Distance cycled from O to A}}{\text{Time taken to cycle from O to A}}$$

$$= \frac{5\text{km}}{0.5\text{h}} = \textbf{10km/h}$$

b) Between A and B there is no movement, i.e. the boy has stopped cycling for 1 hour.

Speed = 0 since there is no slope or gradient.

c) Between B and C the boy is again cycling with constant speed given by the slope or gradient.

$$\text{Speed} = \frac{\text{Distance}}{\text{Time}}$$

$$= \frac{\text{Distance cycled from B to C}}{\text{Time taken to cycle from B to C}}$$

$$= \frac{3\text{km}}{1\text{h}}$$

$$= \textbf{3km/h}$$

Angles

Acute, Right, Obtuse and Reflex Angles

All angles are measured in degrees (°). A protractor can be used to measure the size of an angle.

An angle less than 90° is called an **acute angle**.

An angle equal to 90° is called a **right angle**.

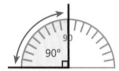 

An angle greater than 90° but less than 180° is called an **obtuse angle**.

An angle greater than 180° is called a **reflex angle**.

 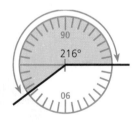

Angles on a Straight Line

Angles on a straight line add up to 180° (also known as Adjacent Angles).

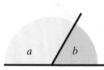
$a = 120°$
$b = 60°$ $a + b = 180°$

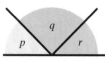
$p = 45°$
$q = 90°$ $p + q + r = 180°$
$r = 45°$

Angles at a Point

Angles at a point add up to 360°.

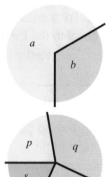
$a = 240°$
$b = 120°$ $a + b = 360°$

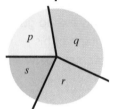
$p = 80°$
$q = 125°$
$r = 90°$ $p + q + r + s = 360°$
$s = 65°$

Vertically opposite angles are equal.

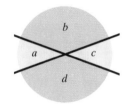
$a = 40°$
$c = 40°$ } Vertically opposite
$b = 140°$
$d = 140°$ } Vertically opposite

Examples
1 Working out the values of **a** and **b**

$a = 180° - 30° =$ **150°**
(Angles on a straight line add up to 180°)
$b =$ **30°** (Vertically opposite angles are equal)

2 Working out the value of **c**

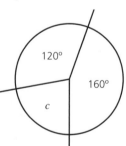

$c = 360° - (120° + 160°)$
$c = 360° - 280° =$ **80°**
(Angles at a point add up to 360°)

Parallel Lines

Parallel lines run in exactly the same direction and never meet. Parallel lines are shown by arrows. There is no limit to the number of lines that may run parallel to each other. When a straight line crosses two or more parallel lines, corresponding and alternate angles are formed.

Alternate Angles

- Alternate angles are formed on opposite (alternate) sides of a line which crosses two or more parallel lines.
- Alternate angles are always equal in size.
- Alternate angles can be easily spotted because they form a letter Z (although sometimes it may be reversed S).

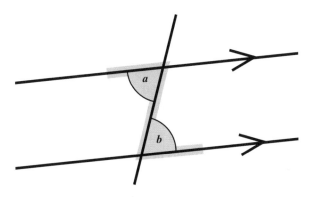

$$\left. \begin{array}{l} a = 70° \\ b = 70° \end{array} \right\} \begin{array}{l} a = b \\ \text{alternate} \\ \text{angles} \end{array}$$

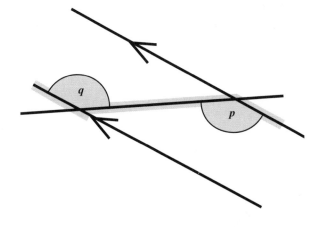

$$\left. \begin{array}{l} p = 145° \\ q = 145° \end{array} \right\} \begin{array}{l} p = q \\ \text{alternate} \\ \text{angles} \end{array}$$

Corresponding Angles

- Corresponding angles are formed on the same side of a line that crosses two or more parallel lines. They all appear in matching (corresponding) positions above or below the parallel lines.
- Corresponding angles are always equal in size.
- Corresponding angles can be easily spotted because they form a letter F (although sometimes it may be reversed, F, or upside down $\mathrm{J,L}$).

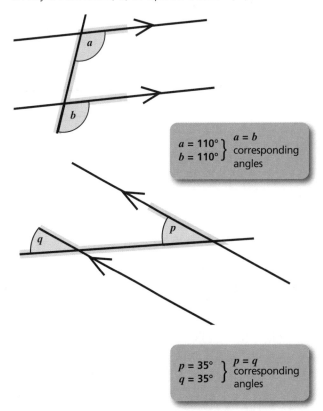

$$\left. \begin{array}{l} a = 110° \\ b = 110° \end{array} \right\} \begin{array}{l} a = b \\ \text{corresponding} \\ \text{angles} \end{array}$$

$$\left. \begin{array}{l} p = 35° \\ q = 35° \end{array} \right\} \begin{array}{l} p = q \\ \text{corresponding} \\ \text{angles} \end{array}$$

Example

Calculate the angles a and b in relation to x in the following parallelogram.

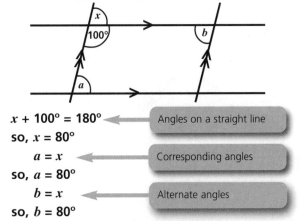

$x + 100° = 180°$ ← Angles on a straight line

so, $x = 80°$

$a = x$ ← Corresponding angles

so, $a = 80°$

$b = x$ ← Alternate angles

so, $b = 80°$

Triangles

Angles in a Triangle

A triangle is a 3-sided two-dimensional shape. The interior angles of the triangle below are a, b and c.

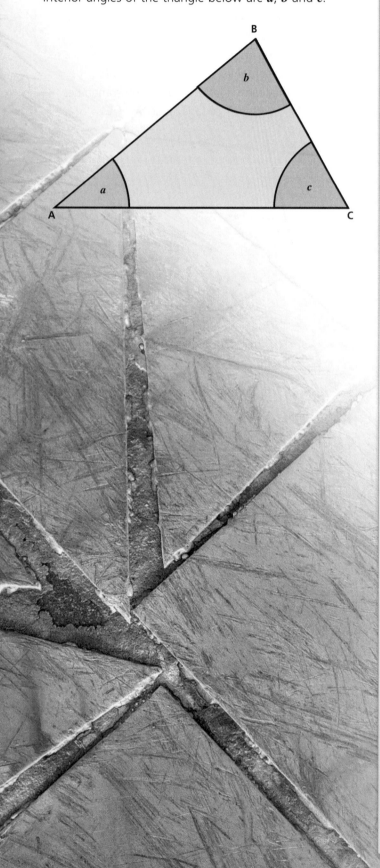

In the triangle below, if we extend the side **AC** to point **D**, and add a line from **C** to **E** which runs parallel to **AB**, then we get the following diagram.

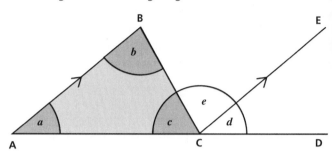

We can now say the following things about these particular angles:

① **The Interior Angles of a Triangle add up to 180°**
From our diagram…

$e = b$ ⟵ Alternate angles

$d = a$ ⟵ Corresponding angles

However…

$c + e + d = 180°$ Angles on a straight line add up to 180°

Therefore, $c + b + a = 180°$, which proves that **the interior angles of a triangle add up to 180°.**

② **The Exterior Angle of a Triangle is equal to the sum of the Interior Angles at the other two vertices.**
The exterior angle of this triangle at the vertex (corner) C is angle BCD. However, we have already shown that:

$e = b$ ⟵ Alternate angles

$d = a$ ⟵ Corresponding angles

Therefore, $d + e = a + b$, which proves that:
the exterior angle of a triangle is equal to the sum of the interior angles at the other two vertices.

Example
Work out the value of x

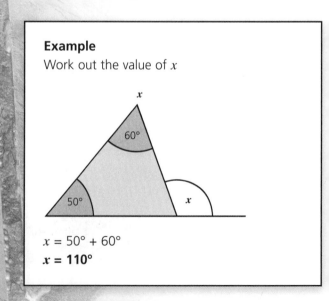

$x = 50° + 60°$

$x = 110°$

Types of Triangle

Right-angled triangles
- One angle is equal to 90°.

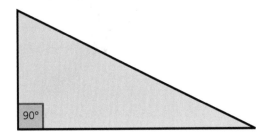

Equilateral triangles
- All sides are equal in length.
- All the angles are equal to 60°.

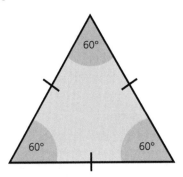

Isosceles triangles
- Only two sides are equal in length.
- Only two angles are equal in size (angles opposite the equal sides).

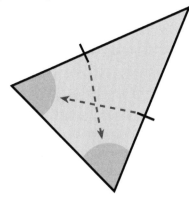

Scalene triangles
- This is the name given to triangles that have no equal sides and no equal angles.

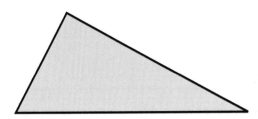

Example
The following diagram shows an isosceles and a right-angled triangle. Calculate the angles a to f explaining your reasoning.

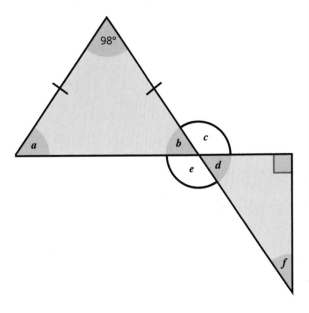

$a = b$ (equal angles in an isosceles triangle)

But, $a + b + 98° = 180°$ (Interior angles of a triangle)

So, $a + b = 82°$ so each one is equal to **41°**.

$b + c = 180°$ (Angles on a straight line)

$c = 180° - 41° = 139°$

$b = d$ (Vertically opposite angles) so, $d = 41°$

$c = e$ (Vertically opposite angles) so, $e = 139°$

$d + f +$ **right-angle $= 180°$**

(Interior angles of a triangle)

So, $f = 180° - 90° - 41° = 49°$

Answer:

$a = 41°$

$b = 41°$

$c = 139°$

$d = 41°$

$e = 139°$

$f = 49°$

Quadrilaterals

Types of Quadrilateral

The interior angles of any quadrilateral add up to 360°.

Square
- All the sides are equal in length.
- Opposite sides are parallel.
- All the angles are equal to 90°.
- Diagonals are equal and bisect each other at right-angles.
- Diagonals also bisect each of the interior angles.

Parallelogram
- Opposite sides are equal in length.
- Opposite sides are parallel.
- Opposite angles are equal in size.
- Diagonals bisect each other.

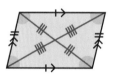

Rhombus
- All the sides are equal in length.
- Opposite sides are parallel.
- Opposite angles are equal in size.
- Diagonals bisect each other at right-angles.
- Diagonals also bisect the interior angles.

Rectangle
- Opposite sides are equal in length.
- Opposite sides are parallel.
- All the angles are equal to 90°.
- Diagonals are equal and bisect each other.

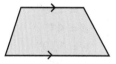

Trapezium
- One pair of sides are parallel.

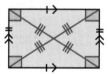

Kite
- 2 pairs of equal adjacent sides.
- 1 pair of opposite equal angles.
- Diagonals cross at right-angles and one bisects the other.

The Interior Angles of a Quadrilateral

> ### Example
> In this quadrilateral…
> $$a = 63°, b = 106°, c = 145°, d = 46°$$
> If we add these together…
> $$63° + 106° + 145° + 46° = \mathbf{360°}$$
>
>

The sum of four angles in a quadrilateral willl always equal 360° and can be proved by dividing the quadrilateral into 2 triangles.

> ### Example
> $$p + q + r = 180° \text{ (Interior angles of a triangle)}$$
> $$s + t + u = 180° \text{ (Interior angles of a triangle)}$$
> The sum of the interior angles of the quadrilateral is
> $(p + s) + q + (r + t) + u$ which is therefore equal to $(p + q + r) + (s + t + u)$,
> i.e. $\mathbf{180° + 180° = 360°}$
>
>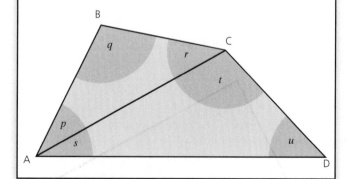

Irregular Polygons

Polygons

A polygon is a two-dimensional shape with 3 or more sides. We have already seen the 3-sided polygon (triangle) and the 4-sided polygon (quadrilateral). A polygon is said to be regular if all its sides and all its angles are equal. Otherwise it is known as an irregular polygon. Take a look at the two irregular polygons on this page.

Interior and Exterior Angles of a Polygon

The angles inside a polygon are called the interior angles and those outside are called the exterior angles. As for triangles and quadrilaterals, the size of each of these angles can be measured using a protractor.

Examples

1

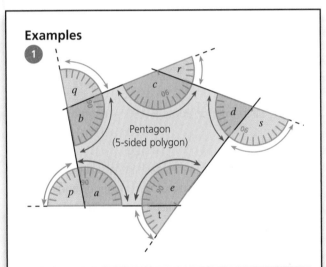

Pentagon (5-sided polygon)

Interior Angles	Exterior Angles	Interior + Exterior Angles
$a = 100°$	$p = 80°$	$a + p = 180°$
$b = 100°$	$q = 80°$	$b + q = 180°$
$c = 140°$	$r = 40°$	$c + r = 180°$
$d = 70°$	$s = 110°$	$d + s = 180°$
$e = 130°$	$t = 50°$	$e + t = 180°$
$a+b+c+d+e$ = 540°	$p+q+r+s+t$ = 360°	

2

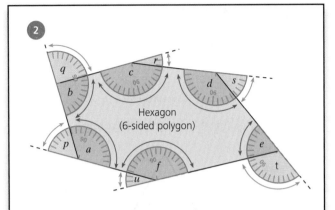

Hexagon (6-sided polygon)

Interior Angles	Exterior Angles	Interior + Exterior Angles
$a = 121°$	$p = 59°$	$a + p = 180°$
$b = 89°$	$q = 91°$	$b + q = 180°$
$c = 158°$	$r = 22°$	$c + r = 180°$
$d = 136°$	$s = 44°$	$d + s = 180°$
$e = 63°$	$t = 117°$	$e + t = 180°$
$f = 153°$	$u = 27°$	$f + u = 180°$
$a+b+c+d+e+f$ = 720°	$p+q+r+s+t+u$ = 360°	

We can see from these two examples that…
- The exterior angles of a polygon always add up to **360°**
- The interior angle + the exterior angle always add up to **180°**

We can also see that the interior angles of different polygons do not add up to the same number of degrees. A triangle is 180°, a quadrilateral is 360°, a pentagon is 540° and a hexagon is 720°. The more sides the polygon has, the greater the sum of the interior angles.

**The sum of the interior angles = (n – 2) × 180°
(where n = number of sides)**

Name of Polygon	Number of Sides (n)	Sum of Interior Angles, (n - 2) × 180°	Sum of Exterior Angles
Triangle	3	180°	360°
Quadrilateral	4	360°	360°
Pentagon	5	540°	360°
Hexagon	6	720°	360°

Regular Polygons

Regular Polygons

Regular polygons have:

- all sides of the same length
- all interior angles of the same size
- all exterior angles of the same size

Here are four examples of regular polygons.

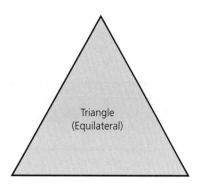

Triangle
(Equilateral)

Quadrilateral
(Square)

Pentagon

Hexagon

Examples

① Calculate the size of **a)** each exterior, and **b)** each interior angle for a regular hexagon (6 sides).

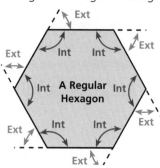

A regular hexagon has 6 equal interior angles and 6 equal exterior angles.

a) The exterior angles of a hexagon add up to 360°

Each exterior angle $= \dfrac{360°}{6} = \mathbf{60°}$

b) The interior angle + the exterior angle add up to 180°

Each interior angle $= 180° -$ exterior angle
$= 180° - 60°$
$= \mathbf{120°}$

② A regular polygon has each interior angle = 108°. Calculate **a)** the size of each exterior angle, and **b)** the number of sides the polygon has.

a) The interior angle + the exterior angle add up to 180°.

Each exterior angle $= 180° -$ interior angle
$= 180° - 108° = \mathbf{72°}$

b) The exterior angles of a Polygon add up to 360° (see previous page)

Number of exterior angles $= \dfrac{360°}{72°} = 5$

Number of sides = 5
(i.e. it is a regular Pentagon)

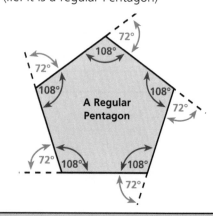

Line or Reflective Symmetry

A two-dimensional shape has a **line of symmetry** if it can be 'cut in half' so that one half of the shape is an exact mirror image of the other half of the shape.

The shapes below have 1 line of symmetry. These shapes can be 'cut in half' only once, and one half of the shape is congruent to the other half.

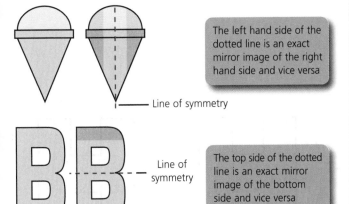

The left hand side of the dotted line is an exact mirror image of the right hand side and vice versa

———— Line of symmetry

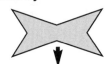

Line of symmetry

The top side of the dotted line is an exact mirror image of the bottom side and vice versa

It is also possible for shapes to have more than 1 line of symmetry. A simple way to find lines of symmetry is to use tracing paper.

Two Lines of Symmetry

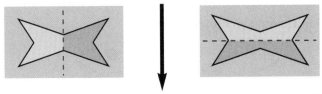

Draw in where you think the line of symmetry is and trace one side of your shape carefully on the tracing paper.

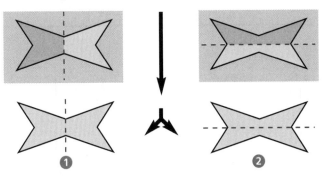

Flip the tracing paper over about the line of symmetry. If your line of symmetry is correct you should get an exact mirror image.

Three Lines of Symmetry

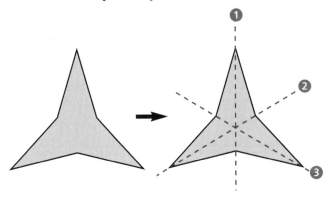

Four Lines of Symmetry

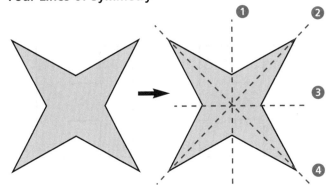

Some shapes, especially regular polygons, can have even more lines of symmetry. However, there are shapes that have **no line of symmetry**. The shapes below cannot be 'cut in half' to give exact mirror images.

Symmetry

Rotational Symmetry

A two-dimensional shape has **rotational symmetry** if it can be 'rotated about a point', called the centre of rotation, to a different position where it looks the same as it was to begin with. The order of rotational symmetry is equal to the number of times a shape fits onto itself in one 360° turn.

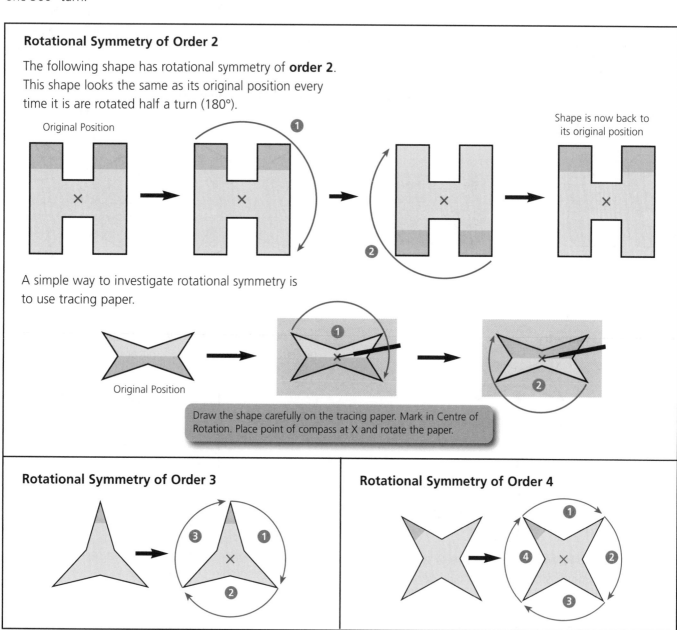

Rotational Symmetry of Order 2

The following shape has rotational symmetry of **order 2**. This shape looks the same as its original position every time it is are rotated half a turn (180°).

Original Position

Shape is now back to its original position

A simple way to investigate rotational symmetry is to use tracing paper.

Original Position

Draw the shape carefully on the tracing paper. Mark in Centre of Rotation. Place point of compass at X and rotate the paper.

Rotational Symmetry of Order 3

Rotational Symmetry of Order 4

Some shapes, especially regular polygons, can have rotational symmetry of even higher orders. However, there are shapes that have **rotational symmetry of order 1** (this can also be referred to as **no rotational symmetry**). These shapes only look the same as their original position when they have been rotated one complete turn (360°).

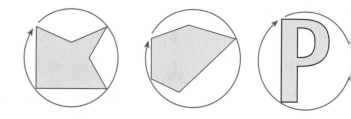

Congruence & Tessellation

Congruent Shapes

The pictures of the boys are **identical** in their **size** and **shape** although their position relative to each other may be different. The pictures of the four boys are **congruent**.

Examples

1 These four shapes are congruent:

This is our original shape:

This is our original shape, turned slightly clockwise:

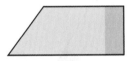

This is our original shape, back to front:

This is our original shape, turned upside down and turned slightly anti-clockwise:

2

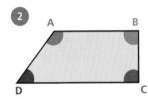 

Shape **ABCD** and shape **PQRS** are congruent so,
$\hat{A} = \hat{P}$, $\hat{B} = \hat{Q}$, $\hat{C} = \hat{R}$ and $\hat{D} = \hat{S}$.

Two congruent shapes have angles the same size and sides of the same length, so **AB = PQ**, **BC = QR**, **CD = RS** and **DA = SP**.

Tessellations

A **tessellation** is a pattern of **congruent shapes** that fit together with **no gaps in between** to cover a flat surface. Your kitchen floor may well be a tessellation.

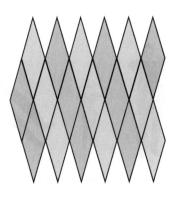

Not all congruent shapes form a tessellation. Two or more additional congruent shapes may be needed to form a tessellation.

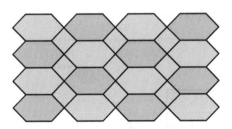

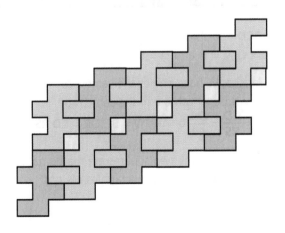

Similarity

Similar Shapes

The pictures of these boys are **identical** in their **shape** but they are **not identical** in size (they can be bigger or smaller). Yet again their position relative to each other may be different. The pictures of these four boys are **similar**.

Example

These four shapes are similar:
This is our original shape:

This is our original shape, but bigger in size:

This is our original shape, but smaller in size:

This is our original shape, smaller in size, upside down and turned slightly clockwise:

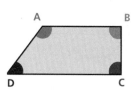

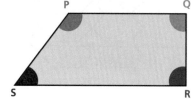

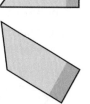

Shape **ABCD** and shape **PQRS** are **similar** because $\hat{A} = \hat{P}, \hat{B} = \hat{Q}, \hat{C} = \hat{R}$ and $\hat{D} = \hat{S}$.

Two similar shapes have angles the same size – and they have sides whose length are in the same ratio, so

$$\frac{AB}{PQ} = \frac{BC}{QR} = \frac{CD}{RS} = \frac{DA}{SP} \text{ or } AB:PQ = BC:QR = CD:RS = DA:SP$$

Any two circles and any two squares are mathematically similar, while **in general**, two rectangles are not.

Examples

The two triangles below are similar.

Calculate the length of…

a) QR

b) AC

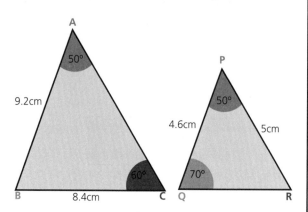

In triangle ABC, $\hat{B} = 70°$ ($180° - (60° + 50°)$) and in triangle PQR, $\hat{R} = 60°$ ($180° - (70° + 50°)$).

And so $\hat{A} = \hat{P}, \hat{B} = \hat{Q}, \hat{C} = \hat{R}$.

This means that triangle ABC is similar to triangle PQR, which means that…

$$\frac{AB}{PQ} = \frac{BC}{QR} = \frac{AC}{PR}$$

> Don't assume that the shapes (in this case triangles) are always lettered in alphabetical order

$$\frac{9.2cm}{4.6cm} = \frac{8.4cm}{QR} = \frac{AC}{5cm}$$

We can now calculate the unknown lengths…

a) $\frac{9.2cm}{4.6cm} = \frac{8.4cm}{QR}$

$$QR = \frac{8.4cm \times 4.6cm}{9.2cm}$$

> Rearranged to get QR on its own

$$QR = 4.2cm$$

b) $\frac{9.2cm}{4.6cm} = \frac{AC}{5cm}$

$$AC = \frac{9.2cm \times 5cm}{4.6cm}$$

> Rearranged to get AC on its own

$$AC = 10cm$$

Pythagoras' Theorem

Pythagoras

Pythagoras was a Greek philosopher and mathematician who lived over 2000 years ago. His theorem is used to calculate the length of an unknown side in a right-angled triangle when the lengths of the other two sides are known. The theorem states… **'the square on the Hypotenuse of a right-angled triangle is equal to the sum of the squares on the other two sides'**.

This is shown in our diagram. The square on the hypotenuse (the longest side, always found opposite the right-angle) is 25, which is the sum of the squares on the other two sides (16 + 9). This can be summarised using the formula $c^2 = a^2 + b^2$. Often, you are asked to work out the length of the hypotenuse (c). In our diagram, we know that $c^2 =$ **25 squares**. So, if you remember powers and roots (pages 14 – 16)… $c^2 = 25$ and so $c = \sqrt{25} = 5$ **units**.

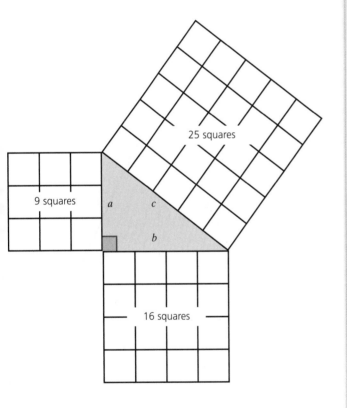

Examples

1 Calculate the length of c in the following right-angled triangle.

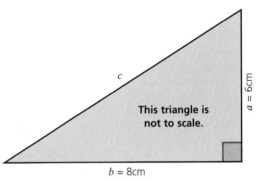

This triangle is not to scale.

$a = 6$cm
$b = 8$cm

Using Pythagoras' Theorem
$c^2 = a^2 + b^2$
$c^2 = 6^2 + 8^2$
$c^2 = 36 + 64$
$c^2 = \mathbf{100}$

To get c we need to take the square root.
$c = \sqrt{100}$
$c = \mathbf{10}$**cm** (remember the units)

2 Calculate the length of c in the following right-angled triangle to 1 decimal place.

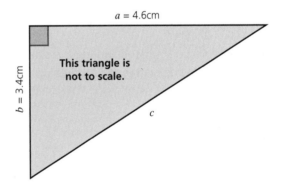

$a = 4.6$cm
$b = 3.4$cm

This triangle is not to scale.

Using Pythagoras' Theorem
$c^2 = a^2 + b^2$
$c^2 = 4.6^2 + 3.4^2$
$c^2 = 21.16 + 11.56$
$c^2 = \mathbf{32.72}$

To get c we need to take the square root.

$c = \sqrt{32.72}$
$c = \mathbf{5.7}$**cm** (remember the units)

Pythagoras' Theorem

Using Pythagoras' Theorem to Calculate the Length of One of the Shorter Sides

So far we have used Pythagoras' Theorem to find the square and length of the hypotenuse. It can also be used to calculate the square and length of one of the shorter sides.

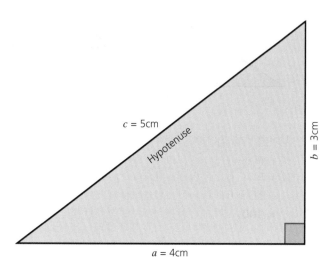

If we look at our formula $c^2 = a^2 + b^2$, it can be rearranged to make a^2 or b^2 the subject:

$$a^2 = c^2 - b^2$$
$$b^2 = c^2 - a^2$$

We can check this works by substituting the side lengths on our diagram into the rearranged formula.

$a^2 = c^2 - b^2$
$4^2 = 5^2 - 3^2$
16 = 25 – 9 ✓

$b^2 = c^2 - a^2$
$3^2 = 5^2 - 4^2$
9 = 25 – 16 ✓

The square on one of the shorter sides	=	The square on the Hypotenuse	–	The square on the other short side

Examples

1 Calculate the length of b in the following right-angled triangle.

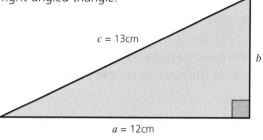

Using Pythagoras' Theorem rearranged
$b^2 = c^2 - a^2$
$b^2 = 13^2 - 12^2$
$b^2 = 169 - 144$
$b^2 = 25$

To get b we need to take the square root.
$b = \sqrt{25}$
$b = 5$cm

2 Calculate the height of the isosceles triangle shown below, to 3 significant figures.

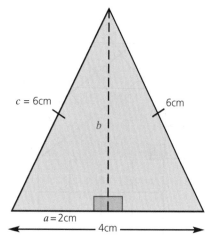

First we must divide the triangle into two right-angled triangles (as shown by the dotted line) in order to use Pythagoras' theorem and label the one we are going to work with (in red).
$b^2 = c^2 - a^2$
$b^2 = 6^2 - 2^2$
$b^2 = 36 - 4$
$b^2 = 32$

To find the height (b) we need to take the square root
$b = \sqrt{32}$ **= 5.66cm**

Perimeter

Perimeter

The perimeter is a measure of the distance all the way around the outside of a shape. All we need to know are the lengths of all the sides that make up the shape and then simply add them together.

Example

1 Calculate the perimeter of this shape.

The lengths of all the sides are given or can be worked out as follows:

Perimeter
= Length of AB + BC + CD + DE + EF + FA
= 6cm + 2.5cm + 4cm + (4.1 - 2.5)cm + 2cm + 4.1cm
= 20.2cm (remember the units)

2 Measure the sides of this triangle and find its perimeter.

Perimeter
= Length of AB + BC + CA
= 6.2cm + 5.7cm + 4.3cm
= 16.2cm (remember the units)

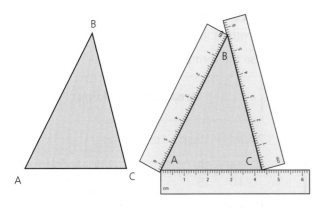
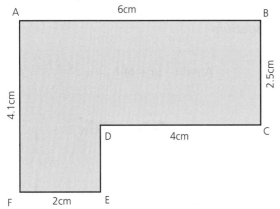

3 Use the grid to workout the perimeter of this shape.

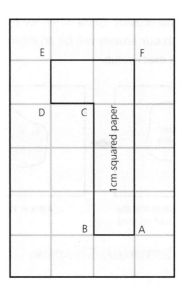

Perimeter
= Length of AB + BC + CD + DE + EF + FA
= 1cm + 3cm + 1cm + 1cm + 2cm + 4cm
= 12cm (remember the units)

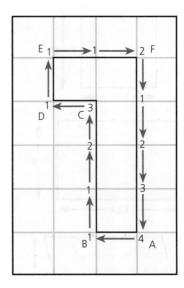

Area

Area

Area is a measure of the amount of surface a two dimensional shape covers. Area is usually measured in **units²**, e.g. **cm²** (cm squared) or **m²** (m squared).

Estimation of Area Using Squared Paper

The area of a shape can be estimated if it has been drawn on squared paper. All we have to do is count the number of squares taken up by the shape.

This method is particularly useful when we have irregular shapes, although our answer will be an estimate of the area and not an exact value.

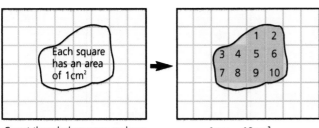

Count the whole squares and any squares more than half covered

Area = 10cm²

Areas of Common Shapes

The following shapes each have a formula which can be used to work out their area exactly.

Area = Base × Height

Square

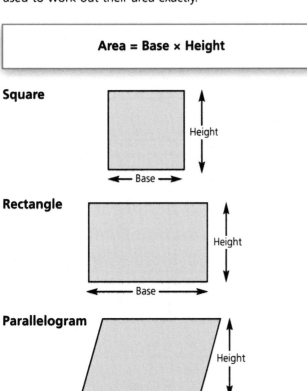
Height · Base

Rectangle

Height · Base

Parallelogram

Height · Base

Triangle

$$\text{Area} = \frac{1}{2}\,\text{base} \times \text{height} \text{ or } = \frac{\text{base} \times \text{height}}{2}$$

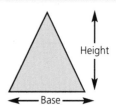

Height · Base

Trapezium

$$\text{Area} = \frac{1}{2}(a + b)\,h \text{ or } = \frac{(a + b)}{2} \times h$$

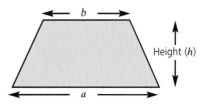

b · Height (h) · a

Examples

1 Calculate the area of the following trapezium.

Use the formula:

6m · 4m · 10m

$$\text{Area} = \frac{(a + b)}{2} \times \text{Height}$$

$$\text{Area} = \frac{(10 + 6)}{2} \times 4 = \frac{16}{2} \times 4$$

$$= 8 \times 4$$

$$= \mathbf{32m^2} \text{ (remember the units)}$$

2 The following parallelogram has an area of 24cm². Calculate its height if the length of its base is 10cm.

Use the formula:

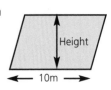
Height · 10m

Area = Base × Height

$$24cm^2 = 10cm \times \text{Height}$$

$$\frac{24}{10} = \frac{10}{10} \times \text{Height}$$

Divide both sides by 10 to give the height on its own

Height = 2.4cm (remember the units)

Area

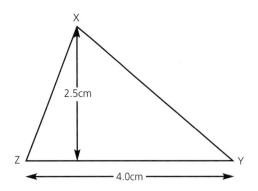

Deducing the Formula for the Area of a Parallelogram

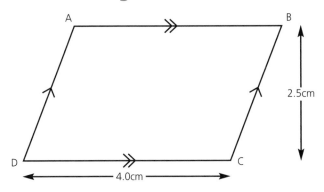

The base of the parallelogram above is 4cm long and the perpendicular height is 2.5cm.

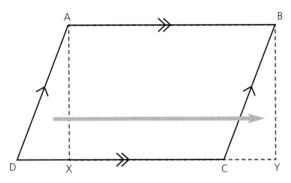

If we cut the triangle **ADX** off one side of the parallelogram and move it to the other side to form **BCY**, we create rectangle **ABYX**, which has exactly the same area as our original parallelogram.

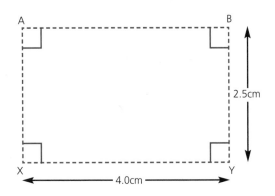

Area of a rectangle = Base × Height
$$= 4 \times 2.5$$
$$= \mathbf{10.0cm^2}$$

Therefore, the formula to work out the area of the parallelogram is:

> **Area of a Parallelogram = Base × Height**

Deducing the Formula for the Area of a Triangle

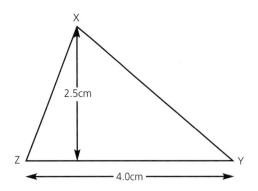

The base of the triangle above is 4cm long and the perpendicular height is 2.5cm.

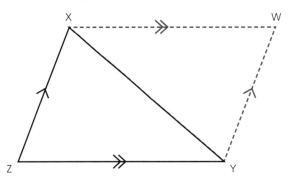

By drawing in the lines XW and WY we create a parallelogram. However, the triangles XYZ and XYW are congruent (the same size and shape), which means that they have equal areas and are, therefore, exactly half of the area of the parallelogram.

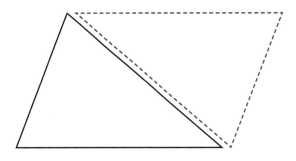

Since the area of a parallelogram is equal to the base multiplied by the height, it follows that:

Area of a triangle $= \dfrac{1}{2} \times$ Base × Height
$$= \dfrac{1}{2}(4 \times 2.5)$$
$$= \mathbf{5.0cm^2}$$

Circles

The following nine diagrams relate to terms used to describe various properties of circles (shown in red). You need to be completely familiar with all of these terms.

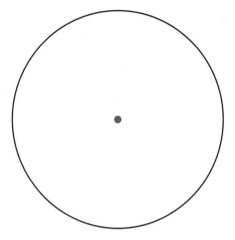

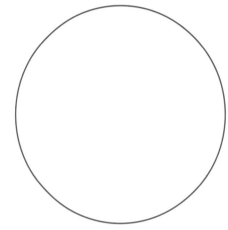

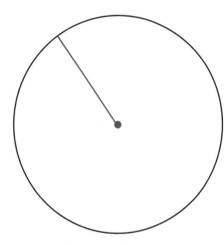

The **centre** of the circle is the only point which is the same distance from every point on the circumference.

The **circumference** is the curve which defines the edge of the circle. Every point on the circumference is the same distance from the centre of the circle.

The **radius** is formed by any straight line drawn from the centre of the circle to the circumference. It is always half the diameter of the circle.

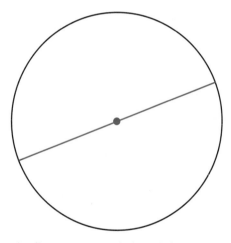

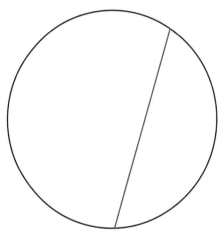

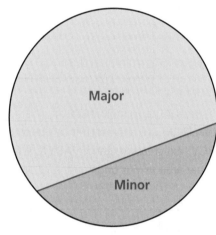

The **diameter** is a straight line which passes through the centre of the circle to join opposite points on the circumference.

A **chord** is a straight line joining two points on the circumference.

Segments are formed by a chord. The larger segment is called the major segment and the smaller one is called the minor segment.

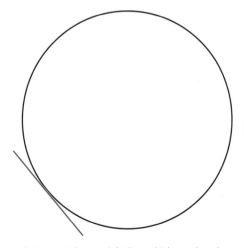

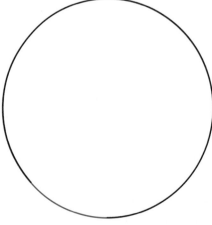

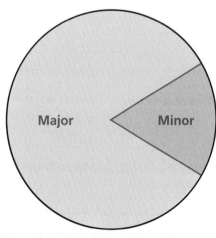

A **tangent** is a straight line which touches the circumference of a circle.

An **arc** is simply part of the circumference of a circle.

A **sector** is the area enclosed by two radii and an arc. It can be major or minor.

Circles

Circumference of a Circle

Circumference is a mathematical word for the perimeter of a circle.

The **radius** is the distance from the centre, •, to the outside of the circle. The **diameter** is the distance from one side of the circle through the centre, •, to the other side of the circle which, therefore, means that:

Length of Radius = $\frac{1}{2}$ × Length of Diameter

or **Length of Diameter = 2 × Length of Radius**

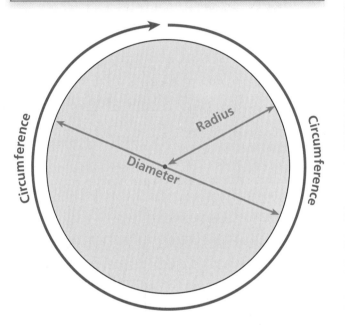

The circumference can be found by using this formula:

Circumference = 2πr or Circumference = πd

where π (called 'pi') has an approximate value of 3.14 and 2πr means 2 × π × r and πd means π × d.

Examples

1 A circle has a radius of **2cm**. Calculate its circumference.

Using our formula...

C = 2πr ← *We use this formula since we are given the **radius***

(using π = 3.14)

= 2 × π × 2cm

= 2 × 3.14 × 2cm

= **12.56cm** (remember the units)

2 A corn circle has a diameter of **20m**. Calculate its circumference.

Using our formula...

C = πd ← *We use this formula since we are given the **diameter***

(using π = 3.14)

C = π × 20m

= 3.14 × 20m

= **62.8m** (remember the units)

Circles & Compound Area

Area of a Circle

The area of a circle is given by the formula...

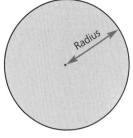

Area = πr^2

Yet again π has a value of 3.14 and πr^2 means $\pi \times$ radius squared or $\pi \times r \times r$. Don't get too worried about π (pi), it's just a different way of saying 3.14.

Example
A circular cricket field has a radius of 80m. Calculate its area (using $\pi = 3.14$).

Using our formula:

Area $= \pi r^2$
$= 3.14 \times 80^2$
$= 3.14 \times 6400$
$= \textbf{20 096m}^2$

Areas of Compound Shapes

Compound shapes are shapes that can be divided up into smaller shapes. The area of each of these smaller shapes can then be calculated and added together.

Example
The diagram shows the layout for a side wall of a house. Calculate its area.

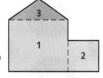

Area of 1 (Rectangle) = 9m × 8m = **72m²**
Area of 2 (Square)   = 3.5m × 3.5m = **12.25m²**
Area of 3 (Triangle) = $\dfrac{9m \times 4m}{2}$ = **18m²**

Area of wall **= Area 1 + Area 2 + Area 3**
        = 72m² + 12.25m² + 18m²
        = **102.25m²**
        (remember the units)

Surface Area of Solids

The surface area of any solid is simply the area of the **net** (see page 82) that can be folded to completely cover the outside of the solid.

Examples
1 Calculate the surface area of the following triangular prism, which has an equilateral triangle as its cross-section.

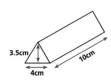

Area of 1 (Rectangle) = 10cm × 4cm = 40cm²
Therefore, Area of 1 + 2 + 3 = 120cm²

Area of 4 (Triangle) = $\dfrac{4cm \times 3.5cm}{2}$ = 7cm²
Therefore, Area of 5 = 7cm²

Surface Area of prism
= Area of 1 + 2 + 3 + 4 + 5
= 120cm² + 7cm² + 7cm²
= **134cm²** (remember the units)

2 Calculate the surface area of this cylinder.

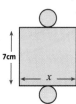

Area of each end = πr^2
        $= 3.14 \times 1.5^2$
        = **7.065cm²**

Radius $= \dfrac{D}{2} = \dfrac{3}{2}$
= 1.5cm

Therefore, both ends
        = 7.065 × 2
        = **14.13cm²**
Length of x = circumference of circle
        = $2\pi r$
        = 2 × 3.14 × 1.5
        = **9.42cm**
Therefore, area of rectangle
        = 7 × 9.42
        = **65.94cm²**
Therefore, total area
        = 14.13cm² + 65.94cm²
        = **80.07cm²**

Transformations

Types of Transformations

A **transformation** is a process which changes the position (and possibly the size and orientation) of a shape. There are four different types of transformation:

- **reflection**
- **rotation**
- **translation**
- **enlargement.**

Reflection

A reflection in a line produces a mirror image in which corresponding points on the original shape and the mirror image are always the same distance from the mirror line. A line joining corresponding points always crosses the mirror line at 90°. To describe a reflection you must specify the **mirror line** by giving the equation of the line of reflection (in the examples below these are $x = 6$ and $y = 1$).

Examples

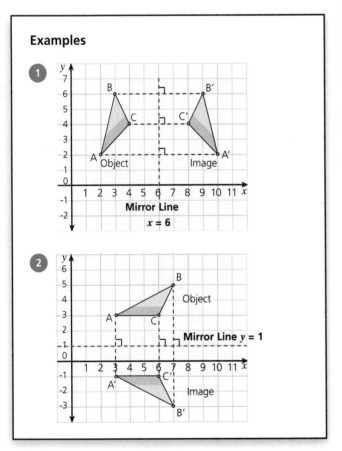

As you can see, in a reflection, the **orientation** and **position** changes but everything else stays the same. Therefore, the image is congruent to the object under a reflection. Difficult reflections can be completed more easily if you use tracing paper. The instruction shown on the right is a reflection in the line $y = -1$.

1. Mark two points (● and ●) on your mirror line.

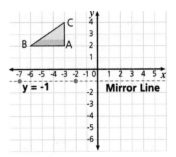

2. Draw in the mirror line, mark points and object carefully on the tracing paper, and then flip the tracing paper over (don't just rotate it!)…

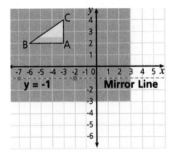

3. … making sure that you line up the mirror line and marked points with the original.

Mark the position of **image** A'B'C'.

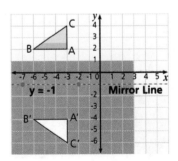

4. Remove the tracing paper.

Draw in **image** and **label** A'B'C'.

An inverted comma (') after the label is used to denote a point on a reflected image.

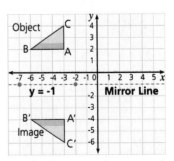

Transformations

Reflection (cont.)

The equation you are given for the mirror line may produce a diagonal line of reflection, e.g. $y = x$.

Example

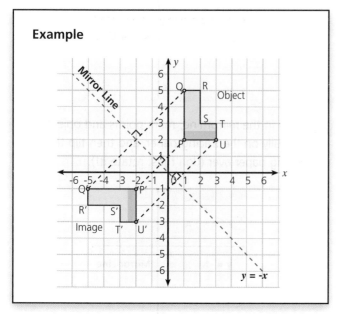

Reflections in diagonal mirror lines are slightly trickier, but if you follow the same basic steps, shown to the right, you should not have a problem.

1 Mark two points (● and ●) on your mirror line.

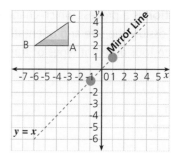

2 Draw in the mirror line, mark points and object carefully on the tracing paper, and then flip the tracing paper over (don't just rotate it!)…

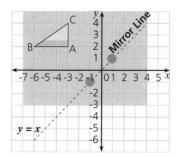

3 … making sure that you line up the mirror line and marked points with the original.

Mark the position of **image** A′B′C′.

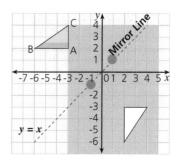

4 Remove the tracing paper.

Draw in **image** and **label** A′B′C′.

An inverted comma (′) after the label is used to denote a point on a reflected image.

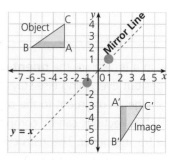

Transformations

Rotation

A rotation turns a shape through a clockwise or anti-clockwise angle about a fixed point known as the Centre of Rotation. All lines in the shape rotate through the same angle. Rotation (just like reflection) changes the **orientation** and **position** of the shape, but everything else stays the same. Therefore the image is congruent to the object under rotation. To describe a rotation, you must specify the following three things:

- The **direction of turn** (clockwise / anti-clockwise)
- The **centre of rotation**
- The **angle turned**

Examples

1 Rotation of $\frac{1}{4}$ turn clockwise about the origin (0,0)

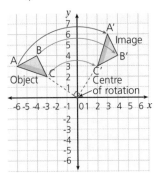

2 Rotation of $\frac{1}{2}$ turn about the origin (0,0)

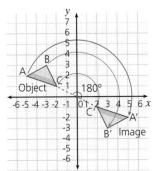

3 Rotation of $\frac{3}{4}$ turn clockwise about the origin (0,0) (is the same as a rotation of $\frac{1}{4}$ anti-clockwise)

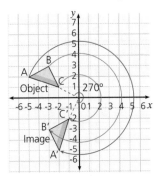

Difficult rotations can be completed more easily if you use tracing paper. If you want to rotate triangle ABC $\frac{1}{4}$ turn clockwise about the origin (0,0) use the following steps:

1 Draw in axes and object carefully on the tracing paper.

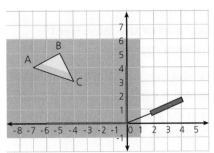

2 Place point of compass on centre of rotation (0,0) and rotate paper clockwise.

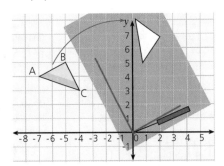

3 After a $\frac{1}{4}$ turn, mark in position of image.

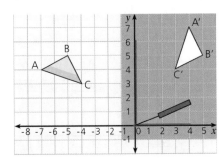

4 Remove the tracing paper. Draw in image and label.

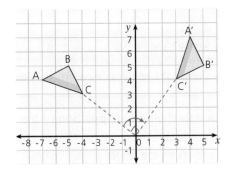

You may be asked to find the centre of rotation when the object and image are shown. Again, you can use tracing paper to test different points until you find the right one.

Transformations

Translation

A translation alters the position of a shape by moving every point of it by the same distance in the same direction. To describe a translation, you must specify the following two things:

- **The direction of the movement**
- **The distance moved**

This can be summarised using brackets in which the movement in the *x* direction is placed directly above the movement in the *y* direction. Positive and negative numbers are used to indicate the direction of the movement.

Examples

ABC has been translated to A''B''C'' by moving 11 squares to the left and then 4 squares down. This translation is written as a vector $\begin{pmatrix} -11 \\ -4 \end{pmatrix}$

ABC has been translated to A'B'C' by moving 7 squares to the right and then 2 squares up. This translation is written as a vector $\begin{pmatrix} 7 \\ 2 \end{pmatrix}$

ABC has been translated to A'''B'''C''' by moving 6 squares to the right and then 7 squares down. This translation is written as a vector $\begin{pmatrix} 6 \\ -7 \end{pmatrix}$

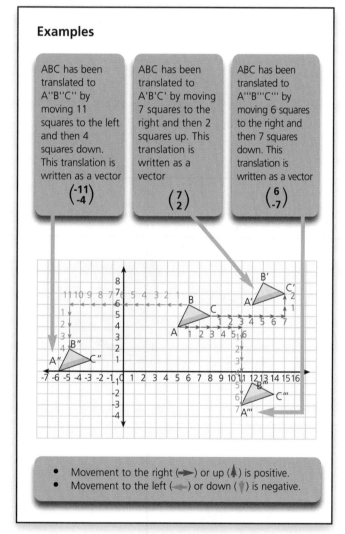

- Movement to the right (→) or up (↑) is positive.
- Movement to the left (←) or down (↓) is negative.

Translation only changes the **position** of the shape. Everything else stays the same, so that any figure is congruent to its image under a translation.

Difficult translations can be completed more easily if you use tracing paper. Notice that all points (P', Q', R', S', T' and U') in the following example have moved 6 to the right and 6 down.

1. This shape must be translated using the translation vector $\begin{pmatrix} 6 \\ -6 \end{pmatrix}$

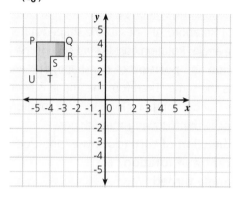

2. Trace the shape onto tracing paper.

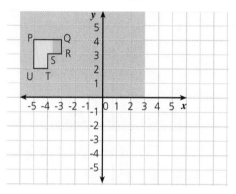

3. Place the tracing paper in the correct position using any point, e.g. P.

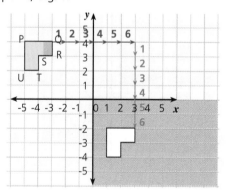

4. Draw over the image, first checking that it is correct.

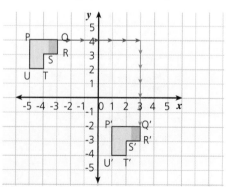

Transformations

Enlargement

An enlargement changes the size of a shape. The shape can be made bigger or smaller according to the scale factor. All enlargements take place from one point called the centre of enlargement.

To describe an enlargement you must specify the following two things:

- **The centre of enlargement**
- **The scale factor**

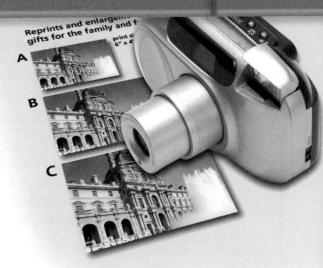

Examples
Enlarge triangle ABC by a scale factor of 2, centre (0,0).

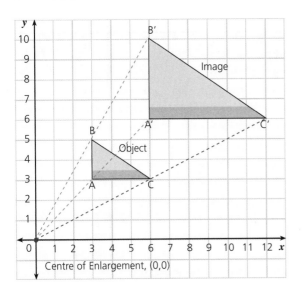

Triangle A'B'C' is an enlargement of triangle ABC by a scale factor of 2, centre (0,0).

A'B' = 2 × AB	OA' = 2 × OA
A'C' = 2 × AC and	OB' = 2 × OB
B'C' = 2 × BC	OC' = 2 × OC

When the centre of enlargement is at (0,0), there is an easy way to find the coordinates of the image.

New coordinates = old coordinates × scale factor

In the example above, A = (3,3) and A' = (6,6) = (3 × 2, 3 × 2)

In the same way B = (3,5) and B' = (6,10) = (3 × 2, 5 × 2) and C = (6,3) and C' = (12,6) = (6 × 2, 3 × 2).

Enlargement only changes the **size** of the shape (i.e. the lengths of its sides) and its **position**.

Sometimes you are asked to calculate the scale factor and find the centre of enlargement.

The scale factor of any enlargement is equal to the ratio of the lengths of any two corresponding sides in the object and the image.

Example
Triangle P'Q'R' is an enlargement of triangle PQR. What is the scale factor of the enlargement and the coordinates of the centre of enlargement?

- **To find the centre of enlargement:**
  Draw dotted lines passing through
  P and P' (_____), Q and Q' (_____), R and R' (_____)
  where these dotted lines cross is the centre of enlargement. **Coordinates are (0, 1).**

- **To find the scale factor of the enlargement:**
  P'Q' = 10 units
  PQ = 2 units
  P'Q' = 5 × PQ.
  Scale Factor of the enlargement is **5**.

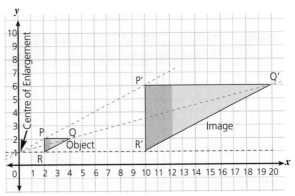

Transformations

Combination of Transformations

Very often a combination of two (or more) transformations can be described by a single transformation.

Examples

1 Triangle ABC is reflected in the y-axis to A'B'C' and then A'B'C' is reflected in the x-axis to A''B''C''. Draw the two transformations and describe fully the single transformation that maps triangle ABC onto triangle A''B''C''.

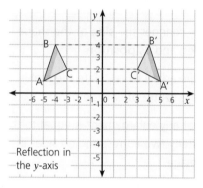

Reflection in the y-axis

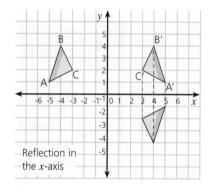

Reflection in the x-axis

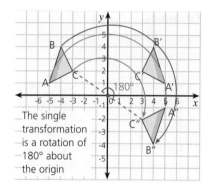

The single transformation is a rotation of 180° about the origin

2 Shape A is rotated 90° clockwise about the origin to shape B. Shape B is then reflected in the x-axis to shape C. Draw the two transformations and describe fully the single transformation that maps shape A onto shape C.

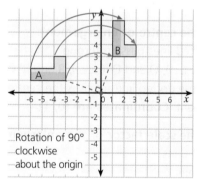

Rotation of 90° clockwise about the origin

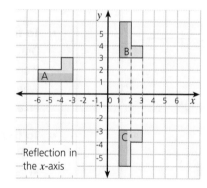

Reflection in the x-axis

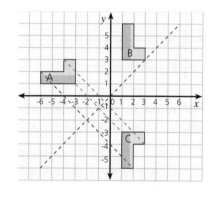

The single transformation is a reflection in the line $y = x$

Characteristics of Transformations – A Summary

Transformation / Characteristic	You need to specify...	Properties that are preserved	Properties that change	Congruent or Similar?
Reflection	• The mirror line (equation of the line of reflection)	Shape and size (e.g. angles, lengths of sides)	Orientation, position	Congruent
Rotation	• Direction of turn • Centre of Rotation • Angle turned through	Shape and size (e.g. angles, lengths of sides)	Orientation, position	Congruent
Translation	• Direction of movement • Distance moved	Shape and size (e.g angles, lengths of sides) and orientation	Position	Congruent
Enlargement	• Centre of Enlargement • Scale Factor	Angles, ratios of lengths of side, orientation	Position, size	Similar

Constructions

Construction of Triangles

In your exams, you must show all construction lines.

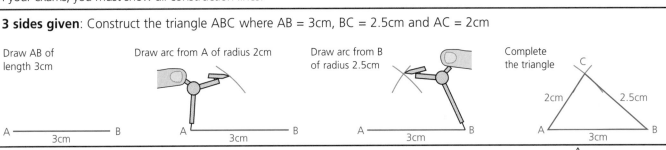

3 sides given: Construct the triangle ABC where AB = 3cm, BC = 2.5cm and AC = 2cm

Draw AB of length 3cm

Draw arc from A of radius 2cm

Draw arc from B of radius 2.5cm

Complete the triangle

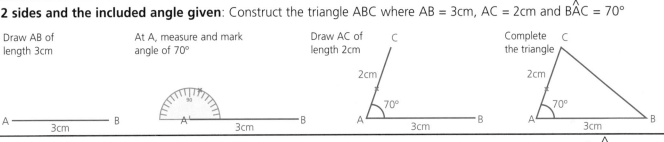

2 sides and the included angle given: Construct the triangle ABC where AB = 3cm, AC = 2cm and $B\hat{A}C = 70°$

Draw AB of length 3cm

At A, measure and mark angle of 70°

Draw AC of length 2cm

Complete the triangle

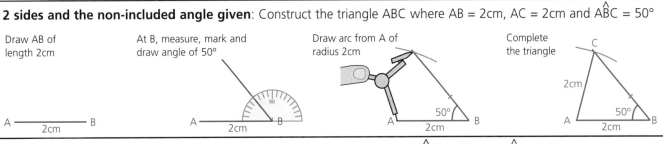

2 sides and the non-included angle given: Construct the triangle ABC where AB = 2cm, AC = 2cm and $A\hat{B}C = 50°$

Draw AB of length 2cm

At B, measure, mark and draw angle of 50°

Draw arc from A of radius 2cm

Complete the triangle

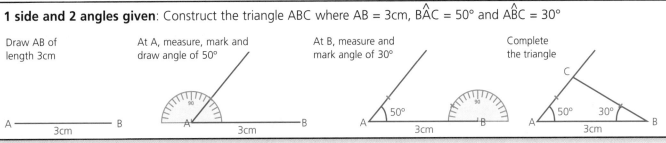

1 side and 2 angles given: Construct the triangle ABC where AB = 3cm, $B\hat{A}C = 50°$ and $A\hat{B}C = 30°$

Draw AB of length 3cm

At A, measure, mark and draw angle of 50°

At B, measure and mark angle of 30°

Complete the triangle

Construction of an Angle of 60° and 90°

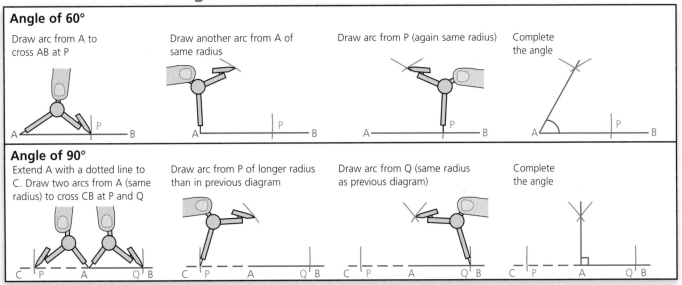

Angle of 60°

Draw arc from A to cross AB at P

Draw another arc from A of same radius

Draw arc from P (again same radius)

Complete the angle

Angle of 90°

Extend A with a dotted line to C. Draw two arcs from A (same radius) to cross CB at P and Q

Draw arc from P of longer radius than in previous diagram

Draw arc from Q (same radius as previous diagram)

Complete the angle

Constructions

The Midpoint and Perpendicular Bisector of a Line Segment

Draw arcs of equal radius from points A and B to intersect at C.

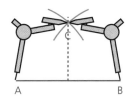

Draw arcs of the same radius on the other side of the line to intersect at D.

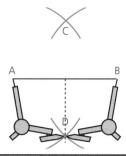

Join C to D to form the perpendicular bisector, (or to locate the midpoint).

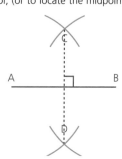

The Perpendicular from a Point to a Line

Draw two arcs from O to cross AB at P and Q.

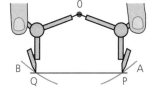

Draw arc from P.

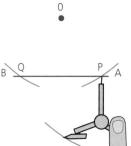

Draw arc from Q (using same radius as previous diagram).

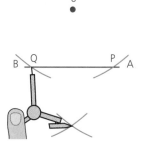

Complete the perpendicular.

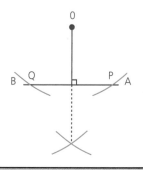

The Perpendicular from a Point on a Line

Draw arcs of equal radius from point O, to cross AB at P and Q.

Draw arcs of the same radius (but greater than step 1) from P and Q to intersect at R.

Join O to R to form the perpendicular from point O.

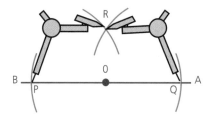

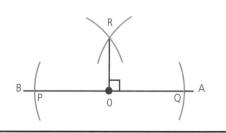

The Bisector of an Angle

This construction may be combined with the construction of angles 60° and 90° to give angles of 30° and 45°.

Draw arcs of equal radius from point A to cut lines at B and C.

Draw arcs of equal radius from points B and C to intersect at point D.

Join A to D to form the bisector of the angle.

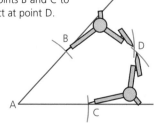

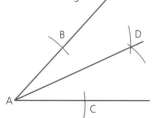

Constructions

Construction of a Regular Hexagon
Inside a Circle

A simple way to construct a regular hexagon inside a circle is as follows:

Show all your construction lines.

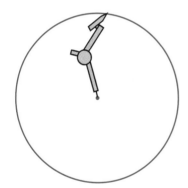

First of all construct the circle with the radius you require.

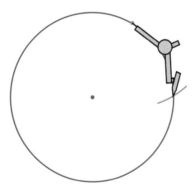

Using the same radius, place the compass point anywhere on the circumference and draw an arc.

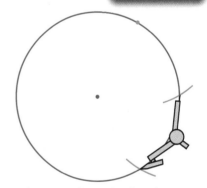

Using the same radius again, place the compass on the point where the arc intersects the circumference and draw another arc.

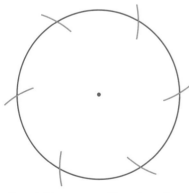

Repeat this process until you have six equal arcs on the circumference of the circle. The final arc should intersect the circumference at your starting point.

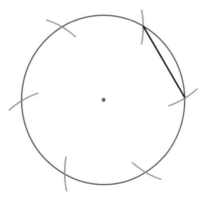

Use a ruler to draw a straight line between the first two points where the arcs intersect the circumference of the circle.

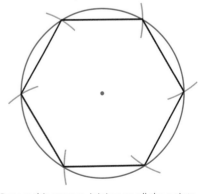

Repeat this process, joining up all the points to form a regular hexagon.

Loci

Locus

A locus is a set of points that follow a given rule. It may be a line, or a curve or a region. You need to know the following loci.

Examples The locus of points which are always at a constant distance from a point is a **circle** whose radius is equal to the constant distance.	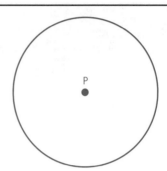
The locus of points which are always at a constant distance from a line is a pair of **parallel lines**, one above and one below the line with a **pair of semi-circles**, one at each end of the line.	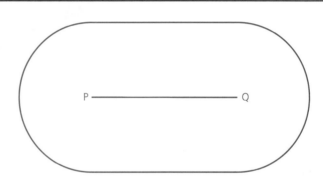
The locus of points which are always equidistant from two points is a **line which bisects the two points at right angles** (i.e. a perpendicular bisector). 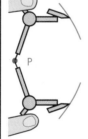	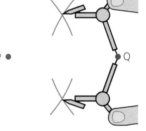 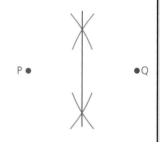 Draw **two** arcs from P Draw **two** arcs from Q (same radius as from P) Draw the line from one intersection of arcs to the other.
The locus of points which are always equidistant from two lines is a line which bisects the angle between the two lines (i.e. an angle bisector). 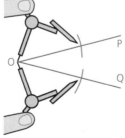	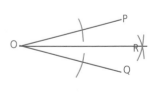 Draw **two** arcs from O to cross the lines OP and OQ Draw **two** arcs from where the first two arcs cross the lines to form point R. Draw the line from R to O to form the angle bisector.

Solids

A solid is a three-dimensional (3-D) shape. A very simple solid is the **cube** (a box with all its sides equal in length).

Vertex (or corner)

Edge

A Hidden Edge (drawn as a dotted line)

Face

Types of Solid

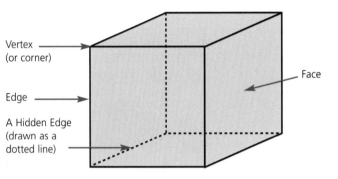

Cuboid

Cylinder

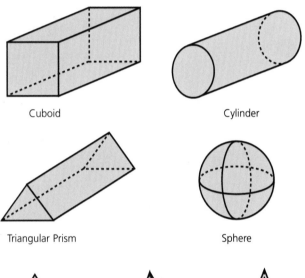

Triangular Prism

Sphere

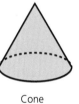

Cone

Square Based Pyramid

Triangular Based Pyramid (Tetrahedron)

Drawing Solids Using Isometric Paper

A disadvantage of drawing solids like the ones above is that accurate measurements of all sides cannot be taken from the diagram. One way of drawing solids is to use isometric paper. This is a grid of equilateral triangles or dots. All solids can be drawn accurately and all measurements can be taken from the diagram.

Examples

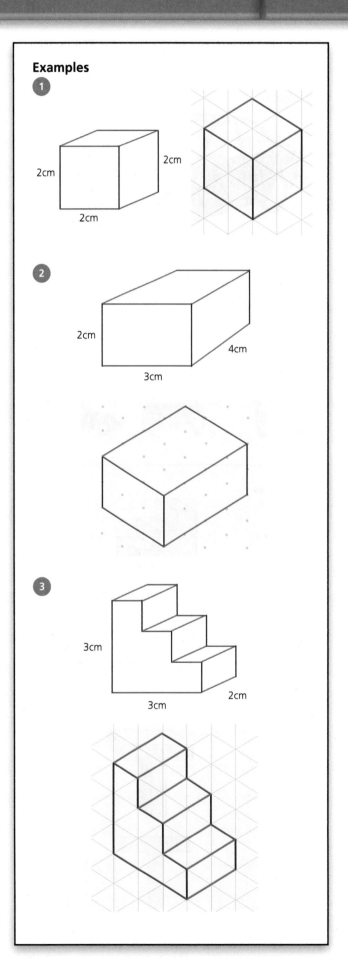

1

2cm

2cm

2cm

2cm

2

2cm

3cm

4cm

3

3cm

3cm

2cm

Nets and Elevations

Plans and Elevations

This is an illustration of a car (a three-dimensional view of a solid).

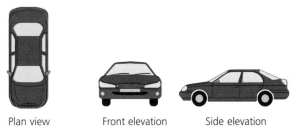

It is possible for us to have three different views of the car:
- **Plan view** where we look down on the car from above.
- **Front elevation** where we look at the car from the front.
- **Side elevation** where we look at the car from the side.

| Plan view | Front elevation | Side elevation |

Examples

1

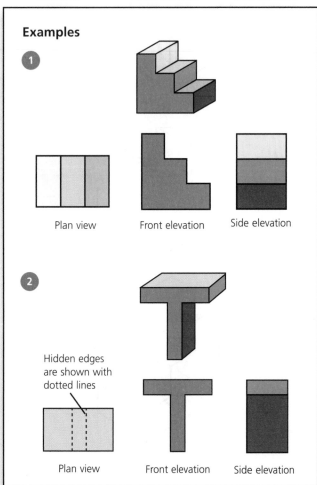

Plan view   Front elevation   Side elevation

2

Hidden edges are shown with dotted lines

Plan view   Front elevation   Side elevation

Nets for Solids

A net is a two-dimensional shape which can be folded to completely cover the outside of a solid.

Examples

1

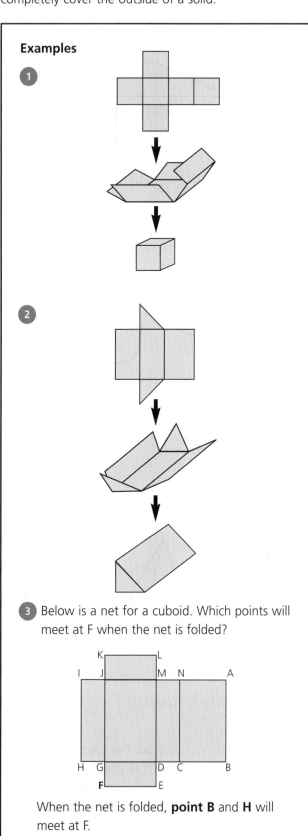

2

3 Below is a net for a cuboid. Which points will meet at F when the net is folded?

When the net is folded, **point B** and **H** will meet at F.

Volume

Volume

Volume is a measure of the amount of space a 3-D object takes up. Volume is usually measured in **units³** e.g. cm cubed (**cm³**) or m cubed (**m³**).

Calculation of the Volume of a Solid Made Up of Cubes

Providing we know the volume of one cube, then all we have to do is work out how many cubes there are in each layer of the solid and then add them up.

Example

In the following example each cube 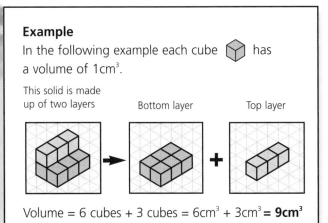 has a volume of 1cm³.

This solid is made up of two layers

Volume = 6 cubes + 3 cubes = 6cm³ + 3cm³ = **9cm³**

Volume of a Cuboid

The volume of a cuboid is given by the formula:

$$\textbf{Volume = Length} \times \textbf{Width} \times \textbf{Height}$$
$$V = l \times w \times h$$

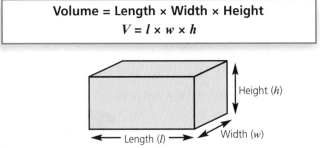

Example

Calculate the volume of the cuboid.

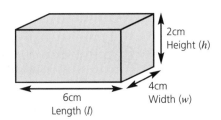

Volume = length × width × height
= 6 × 4 × 2
= **48cm³** (remember the units)

Volume of a Prism

A prism is a solid which has a uniform cross-section from one end of the solid to the other end.

$$\textbf{Volume of a prism}$$
$$\textbf{= Area of cross-section} \times \textbf{Length}$$

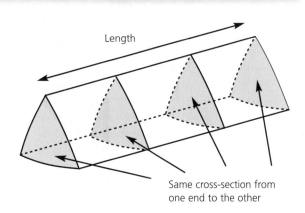

Same cross-section from one end to the other

Example

Calculate the volume of the triangular prism.

The cross-section is a triangle

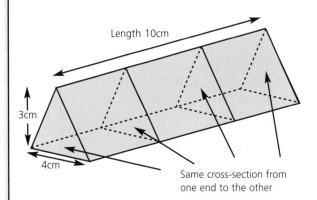

Same cross-section from one end to the other

Using our formula:

Volume = area of cross-section × length

$$= \frac{(\text{base} \times \text{height})}{2} \times \text{length}$$

$$= \frac{(4 \times 3)}{2} \times 10$$

$$= 6\text{cm}^2 \times 10\text{cm}$$

$$= \textbf{60cm}^3 \text{ (remember the units)}$$

Volume

Volume of a Prism (Cont.)

Example

Calculate the volume of this prism.

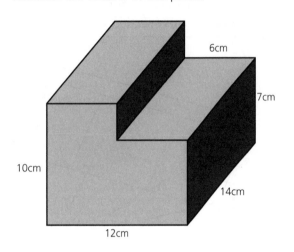

The first step is to find the area of the cross-section.

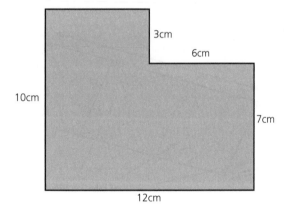

Area = 10 × 12 − 6 × 3
   = 120 − 18
   = 102cm²

Volume = area of cross-section × length
   = 102 × 14
   = 1428cm³

Volume of a Cylinder

A cylinder is a prism which has a uniform cross-section of a circle from one end of the prism to the other. The volume of any cylinder is given by the following formula:

> **Volume of a cylinder = $\pi r^2 l$ = $\pi r^2 \times l$**
> (where l is the length of the cylinder)

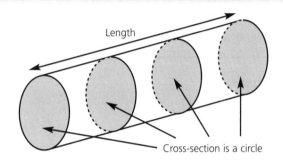

Cross-section is a circle

Examples

1 Calculate the volume of the following cylinder to 2 d.p. (Let π = 3.14)

8cm

2cm

Using our formula:
Volume = $\pi r^2 l$
Volume = $\pi r^2 \times$ length
   = 3.14 × 2² × 8
   = 3.14 × 4 × 8
   = 100.48cm³ (remember the units)

2 A cylindrical tank is 1.6m long and holds 0.8m³ of oil when full. What is the radius of the cylinder to 2 d.p. (Let π = 3.14).

Using our formula:
Volume = $\pi r^2 l$

0.8 = 3.14 × r^2 × 1.6

0.8 = 5.024 × r^2

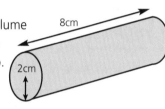

1.6m

$\dfrac{0.8}{5.024} = \dfrac{5.024}{5.024} \times r^2$

> Divide both sides by 5.024 to leave r^2 on its own

0.159 = r^2

$\sqrt{0.159} = \sqrt{r^2}$

> Take square root of both sides to leave r on its own

r = **0.40m**
(remember the units)

Maps & Scale Drawings

Drawing to Size and Scale

Before you attempt to construct any drawing to a particular size or scale you need the following:

- A **pencil** and **rubber** so any mistakes can be rubbed out.
- A **ruler** for drawing straight lines.
- A **protractor** for measuring angles.
- A **compass** for drawing circles, arcs and other constructions

---

Example

Here is a sketch map of an island. The map has four marker points A, B, C and D.

a) Make an accurate scale drawing of the quadrilateral ABCD using a scale of 1cm to represent 10km.

b) Calculate the length of BC.

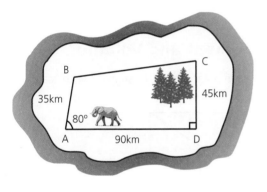

a) Step 1: Draw the 90km line AD (9cm).
   Step 2: Measure and mark 80° and 90°.
   Step 3: Draw the 35km line AB (3.5cm) and the 45km line CD (4.5cm).
   Step 4: Complete the quadrilateral.

b) Length of BC on diagram = 8.4cm.
   Real distance of BC = 8.4 × 10km = **84km**

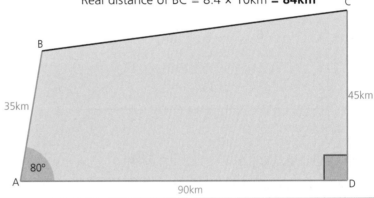

Map Scales

This is part of a map of Devon and Cornwall which is drawn to a scale of 1cm : 10km

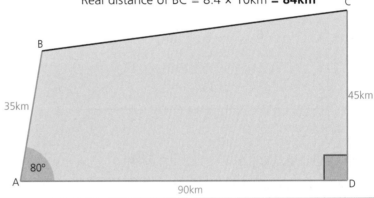

1 The direct distance from Newquay to Plymouth as measured on the map is 7cm. Calculate the actual distance.

Actual distance.

7 × 10 = **70km**

2 The actual direct distance between Torquay and Exeter is 30km. Calculate the map distance.

Map distance.

$\frac{30}{10}$ = **3cm**

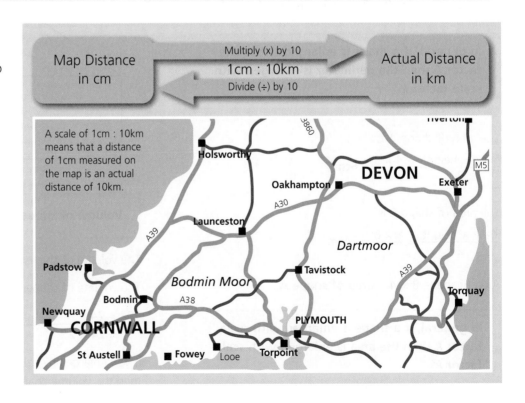

Enlargement, Area, Perimeter & Volume

Enlargement – Perimeter and Area

Shape B is an enlargement of shape A with scale factor 2.

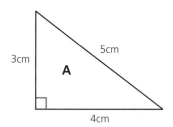

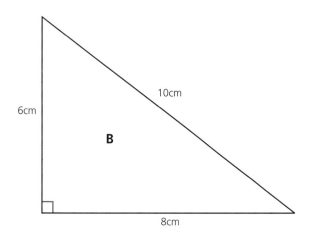

The perimeter of shape A is 3 + 4 + 5 = **12cm**

The perimeter of shape B is 6 + 8 + 10 = **24cm**

Perimeter of shape B **= 2 × perimeter of shape A**

> **In general, if a shape is enlarged with scale factor k then the perimeter is enlarged with scale factor k.**

The area of shape A is:

$$\frac{\text{base × height}}{2} = \frac{4 \times 3}{2} = \textbf{6cm}^2$$

The area of shape B is:

$$\frac{\text{base × height}}{2} = \frac{8 \times 6}{2} = \textbf{24cm}^2$$

Area of shape B **= 4 × area of shape A.**

> **In general, if a shape is enlarged with scale factor k then the area is enlarged with scale factor k^2.**

Enlargement and Volume

Shape Y is an enlargement of shape X with scale factor 2.

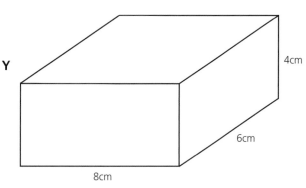

> **Volume of shape Y = volume of shape X × 2^3**

The volume of shape X is 4 × 3 × 2 = **24cm³**

The volume of shape Y is 8 × 6 × 4 = **192cm³**

192 = 24 × 8
   = 24 × 2^3

If you enlarge any solid shape with a scale factor of 2 then the volume changes by a scale factor of 2^3 = 8.

Converting Measurements

Metric and Imperial Units

	Metric Units		Approximate Comparison Between Metric & Imperial		Imperial Units	
Length	10mm	= 1cm	2.5cm ≈	1 inch	12 inches	= 1 foot
	100cm	= 1m	1m ≈	39 inches	3 feet	= 1 yard
	1000m	= 1km	1600m ≈	1 mile	1760 yards	= 1 mile
			8km ≈	5 miles		
Mass	1000mg	= 1g	30g ≈	1 ounce	16 ounces	= 1 pound
	1000g	= 1kg	450g ≈	1 pound	14 pounds	= 1 stone
	1000kg	= 1 tonne	1kg ≈	2.2 pounds		
Capacity or Volume	1000ml	= 1l	1l ≈	$1\frac{3}{4}$ pints	8 pints	= 1 gallon
	1000cm³	= 1l	4.5l ≈	1 gallon		
	(1ml	= 1cm³)				

Converting One Metric Unit to Another

Consider the conversion between centimetres (cm) and metres (m):

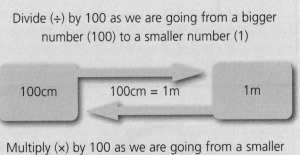

Divide (÷) by 100 as we are going from a bigger number (100) to a smaller number (1)

100cm   100cm = 1m   1m

Multiply (×) by 100 as we are going from a smaller number (1) to a bigger number (100)

Examples

1 Convert 300cm to metres.

From above: cm $\xrightarrow{\div 100}$ m

$300\text{cm} = \dfrac{300}{100} = \textbf{3m}$

2 Penny is 1.65m tall. What is her height in centimetres?

From above: m $\xrightarrow{\times 100}$ cm

$1.65\text{m} = 1.65 \times 100 = \textbf{165cm}$

Converting Between Metric and Imperial Units

These follow the same rules as converting between metric units. Take the conversion between grams (g) and pounds:

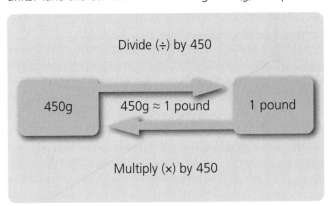

Divide (÷) by 450

450g   450g ≈ 1 pound   1 pound

Multiply (×) by 450

Examples

1 A tin of baked beans has a mass of 600g. What is its mass in pounds?

From above: g $\xrightarrow{\div 450}$ pounds

$600\text{g} = \dfrac{600}{450} = \textbf{1.33 pounds}$ (approx.)

2 A recipe for a cake needs 1.5 pounds of flour. What mass of flour is needed in grams?

From above: pounds $\xrightarrow{\times 450}$ g

$1.5 \text{ pounds} = 1.5 \times 450 = \textbf{675g}$ (approx.)

Bearings

Three-Figure Bearings

A bearing is a measurement of the position of one point relative to another point. It is measured in degrees. **Bearings are always measured from the north in a clockwise direction and are given as 3 digits**. Below are two points, A and B. There are two possible bearings:

- The bearing of B from point A. This means that the measurement of the bearing is taken from point A.
- The bearing of A from point B. This means that the measurement of the bearing is taken from point B.

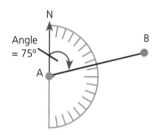

1. Draw in North (N) direction.
2. Measure angle from N direction in a clockwise direction.
3. Angle = 120°.
4. **Bearing of B from A is 120°.**

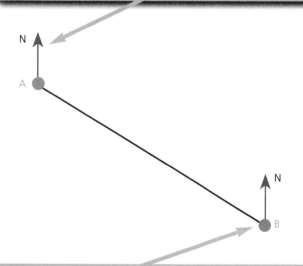

1. Draw in North (N) direction.
2. Measure angle from N direction in a clockwise direction.
3. Angle = 180° + 120° = 300°
4. **Bearing of A from B is 300°.**

A circular protractor with a full 360° range can make three-figure bearings much easier to measure.

Sometimes the angle you measure from the N direction is less than 100° or even less than 10°. In this case one or two zeros are put in front of the angle in order to make them three-figure bearings.

Examples

1. Bearing of B from A is **075°**. (Also bearing of A from B is 255°). Use a protractor to check this bearing.

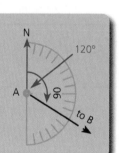

Angle = 75°

2. Bearing of B from A is **007°**. (Also bearing of A from B is 187°). Use a protractor to check this bearing.

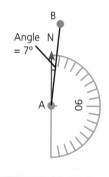

Angle = 7°

Compound Measures

Speed

Speed is a measure of 'how fast' an object is moving. To calculate the speed of a moving object we need two measurements:

- The **distance** it moves.
- The **time** it takes to move that distance.

Speed can be calculated using the formula:

$$\text{Speed } (S) = \frac{\text{Distance } (D)}{\text{Time } (T)}$$

Speed is measured in metres per second (m/s), kilometres per hour (km/h) or miles per hour (mph).

A **formula triangle** makes it a lot easier for us when we want to calculate distance or time.

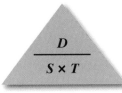

To get the formula for distance, cover 'D' up;
Distance = Speed × Time.

To get the formula for time, cover 'T' up;
Time = $\dfrac{\text{Distance}}{\text{Speed}}$

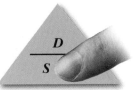

Examples
1. Calculate the speed of a car which travels a distance of 90m in 10s.

   Speed = $\dfrac{90m}{10s}$ = **9m/s** (remember the units)

2. A train completes a journey of 180km at an average speed of 90km/h. How long did the journey take?

   Time = $\dfrac{\text{Distance}}{\text{Speed}}$ = $\dfrac{180km}{90km/h}$ = **2 hours**

Fuel Efficiency

The fuel efficiency of a car is often measured in miles per gallon (mpg).

Cars with higher mpg values are more fuel efficient.

$$\text{Fuel efficiency} = \frac{\text{Number of miles travelled}}{\text{Number of gallons of fuel used}}$$

For example, if a car travels 210 miles on 6 gallons of fuel then its fuel efficiency is given by:

$$\text{Fuel efficiency} = \frac{210}{6}$$

$$= 35\text{mpg}$$

In reality, the numbers are likely to be more difficult to work with and a calculator will be needed.

Example
Mr Smith wants to work out the fuel efficiency of his car. He fills the tank with fuel and writes down the mileage as 45 381. The next time he refuels his car he finds that the mileage has increased to 45 743 and it takes 7.6 gallons of fuel to fill the tank. Calculate the fuel efficiency of Mr Smith's car in mpg (to 1 d.p.).

Number of miles travelled = 45 743 − 45 381 = 362

$$\text{Fuel efficiency} = \frac{362}{7.6}$$

$$= 47.63... \text{ mpg}$$

$$= \textbf{47.6mpg}$$

Measure Lines & Angles

Measuring Lines

The diagram shows a cm ruler and a line to be measured.

Each cm on the ruler is divided into 10 parts, so each part is 0.1cm or 1mm.

The length of the line is 4.2cm to the nearest 0.1cm. This is the same as saying 4.2cm to the nearest mm.

You may need to measure accurately to make a scale drawing or to answer a question on bearings for example.

Measuring Angles

To measure the angle shown below, the first step is to decide whether it is acute or obtuse.

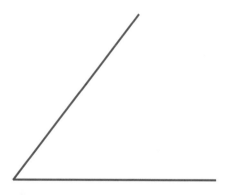

The angle above is acute so, using the protractor, we see it lies between 50° and 60° not between 120° and 130°.

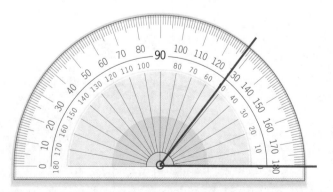

The angle is **52°** to the nearest degree.

The angle shown below is obtuse.

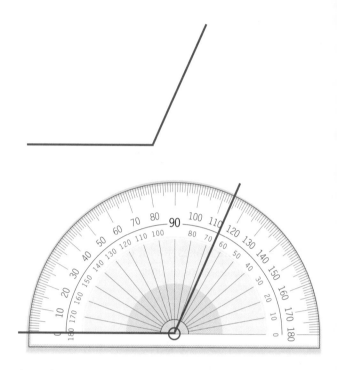

Since the angle is obtuse, it must lie between 110° and 120° not between 60° and 70°. The angle is **114°** to the nearest degree.

The angle shown below is reflex.

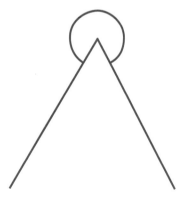

You can only measure a reflex angle directly if you have a 360° protractor.

If you only have a 180° protractor, measure the acute angle between the lines and subtract the value from 360°.

Probability

The Nature of Probability

Probability, quite simply, is a measure of the likelihood of a particular event occurring. Probability is used throughout the world in order to give a sound mathematical basis for predicting future events. These events can be relatively simple such as tossing a coin or spinning a roulette wheel, however, they can also be vastly complicated such as in the assessment of a large insurance risk.

Probability Scale and the Language of Probability

For an event to happen we might say that its probability is 'a certainty', 'more than likely', 'evens' or '50/50', 'not very likely', 'no chance'. The probability of an event occurring (or not occurring) can be stated as either a fraction, percentage or decimal. These can be shown on a probability scale. Here is a very simple one:

These are the only probabilities you can have, i.e. you cannot have a probability greater than 1. So, if the probability of something happening is P, then the probability of it not happening is 1 − P										
0	$\frac{1}{10}$	$\frac{2}{10}$	$\frac{3}{10}$	$\frac{4}{10}$	$\frac{5}{10}$	$\frac{6}{10}$	$\frac{7}{10}$	$\frac{8}{10}$	$\frac{9}{10}$	**1**
0	10%	20%	30%	40%	50%	60%	70%	80%	90%	**100%**
0	0.1	0.2	0.3	0.4	0.5	0.6	0.7	0.8	0.9	**1**

No chance, i.e. impossible	Not very likely	Evens 50/50	More than likely	A certainty, i.e. it must happen

Examples

1 The probability of you passing a maths test is $\frac{7}{10}$. What is the probability that you will fail?

> Since you can only pass or fail, the total probability = 1

P(passing) + P(failing) = 1

$$P(failing) = 1 - P(passing)$$
$$= 1 - \frac{7}{10}$$
$$= \frac{3}{10}$$

This means that you are not very likely to fail!

2 A drawer contains white, black and red socks only. If the probability of picking a white sock at random is 0.2 and a black sock is 0.3, what is the probability of picking a red sock?

> Since the drawer only contains white, black and red socks, the total probability = 1

P(w) + P(b) + P(r) = 1

$$P(r) = 1 - (P(w) + P(b))$$
$$= 1 - (0.2 + 0.3)$$
$$= 1 - 0.5$$
$$= 0.5$$

This means that you have an even chance of picking a red sock at random.

Probability

The Language of Probability

To gain a good understanding of probability you need to learn the vocabulary used to describe it. This section develops the basic vocabulary within the context of examples.

Equally Likely Outcomes

The 12 coloured counters shown below are put into a bag and one is selected without looking.

Since the counters are the same size and shape, each one has an **equal chance** of being selected. The selection of a particular counter is called an **outcome**. In this case, there are 12 **equally likely outcomes** and we say that a counter is to be selected at **random**.

There are 5 red counters so 5 of the possible outcomes are associated with the **event** of selecting a red counter from the 12. In general, an event involves some set of outcomes and we talk about the probability of an event, written as P(event).

When all of the outcomes are equally likely, the probability of an event is given by:

$$P(\text{event}) = \frac{\text{Number of outcomes in the event}}{\text{The total number of outcomes}}$$

Using R to represent the selection of a red counter:

$P(R) = \dfrac{5}{12}$

In the same way, $P(B) = \dfrac{4}{12}$ and $P(Y) = \dfrac{3}{12}$

Notice that;

$P(R) + P(B) + P(Y) \quad = \dfrac{5}{12} + \dfrac{4}{12} + \dfrac{3}{12}$

$\qquad\qquad\qquad\qquad = \dfrac{12}{12} = \mathbf{1}$

The sum of the probabilities of a complete set of mutually exclusive outcomes is always 1

When a fair dice is thrown there are six equally likely outcomes 1, 2, 3, 4, 5 and 6.

These outcomes are mutually exclusive – only one of them can occur on any throw.

$P(1) = \dfrac{1}{6}$ $\qquad\qquad$ $P(4) = \dfrac{1}{6}$

$P(2) = \dfrac{1}{6}$ $\qquad\qquad$ $P(5) = \dfrac{1}{6}$

$P(3) = \dfrac{1}{6}$ $\qquad\qquad$ $P(6) = \dfrac{1}{6}$

The sum of these probabilities is $\dfrac{6}{6} = \mathbf{1}$

Example

The probability that a biased coin lands Heads up is 0.4. What is the probability that the coin lands Tails up?

H and T make a complete set of mutually exclusive outcomes.

$P(H) + P(T) = 1$

$0.4 + P(T) = 1$

$P(T) = 1 - 0.4$

$\mathbf{P(T) = 0.6}$

The probability that the coin lands Tails up is 0.6

Probability

Outcomes of Single Events

- Tossing a coin. Here there are only two outcomes: Heads or Tails
- Throwing a die. Here there are only six outcomes: One, Two, Three, Four, Five or Six

In cases like these, all you have to do is make a simple list.

Outcomes of Two Successive Events

1 **Tossing two coins, one after the other.**

Here, it is easier to use a sample space diagram to show the possible outcomes. With two coins there are 4 outcomes. The chances of each outcome occurring are:

P(Head + Head) = $\frac{1}{4}$

P(Tail + Tail) = $\frac{1}{4}$

P(Head + Tail) = $\frac{1}{4}$

P(Tail + Head) = $\frac{1}{4}$

Note that once again the probabilities add up to make 1,

i.e. $\frac{1}{4} + \frac{1}{4} + \frac{1}{4} + \frac{1}{4} = 1$

Sample Space Diagram

	First coin	
	H	T
H	HH	TH
T	HT	TT

Second coin

2 **Throwing a pair of dice.**

In this case, each die has six possible outcomes. The sample space diagram below, which shows the scores of the two dice added together, reveals a total of 36 possible outcomes. Each outcome (e.g. throwing a 4 with the first die and a 2 with the second) has a $\frac{1}{36}$ probability.

However, while there is only a $\frac{1}{36}$ chance of scoring a total of 2 and the same for scoring 12, there is a $\frac{6}{36}$ or $\frac{1}{6}$ chance of scoring a seven.

Sample Space Diagram

First die

	1	2	3	4	5	6
1	2	3	4	5	6	7
2	3	4	5	6	7	8
3	4	5	6	7	8	9
4	5	6	7	8	9	10
5	6	7	8	9	10	11
6	7	8	9	10	11	12

Second die

Probability

Theoretical Probability

Since the chance of a coin landing on Heads is $\frac{1}{2}$, then the number of Heads we should expect in 10 tosses is...

$$\frac{1}{2} \times 10 = 5$$

The most likely number is heads = 5, but this is not certain.

Relative Frequency

A simple experiment was carried out where a coin was tossed 10, 100 and a 1000 times. The graphs below show the number of Heads and Tails obtained. In theory we would expect to always get the same number of Heads and Tails because the probability of each event occurring is $\frac{1}{2}$ or 0.5

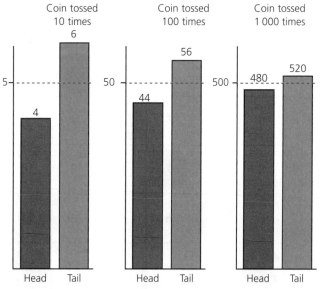

Coin tossed 10 times · Coin tossed 100 times · Coin tossed 1 000 times

The relative frequency of obtaining heads in an experiment is given by:

$$\text{Relative Frequency} = \frac{\text{Number of Heads we get}}{\text{Total number of times the coin was tossed}}$$

If we go back to our experiment, as we increase the number of times the coin is tossed, the relative frequency gets closer and closer to the theoretical probability (red dotted line), e.g. 0.5 for a Head, 0.5 for a Tail.

Theoretical probability relies on equally likely outcomes. If this is not the case, such as when a coin is biased, we must use relative frequency to estimate probability.

	Coin tossed 10 times	Coin tossed 100 times	Coin tossed 1000 times
Relative Frequency	Head = $\frac{4}{10}$ = 0.4	Head = $\frac{44}{100}$ = 0.44	Head = $\frac{480}{1000}$ = 0.48
	Tail = $\frac{6}{10}$ = 0.6	Tail = $\frac{56}{100}$ = 0.56	Tail = $\frac{520}{1000}$ = 0.52

Importance of Sample Size

As you can see from the data above, the bigger the sample, the more reliable it is. It is quite possible that tossing a coin ten times could produce 2 tails and 8 heads, for example. A larger sample would give a more reliable result.

This has implications in testing for **bias**. For instance it would be possible to test experimentally the frequency of red and black on a roulette wheel.

If there was time to take a big enough sample then it would be possible to say with some justification that the wheel wasn't fair, e.g. if 50 000 spins produce 26 750 reds and 23 250 blacks!

Problem Solving & Handling Data

Problem Solving in Statistics

You need to be aware of the problem solving process
in statistics and how to use the
handling data cycle.

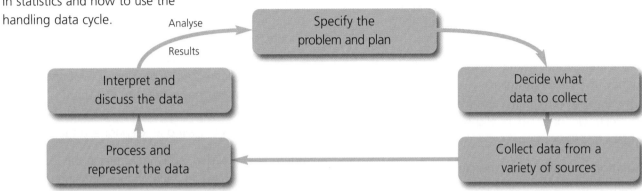

Stage	Examples
Specify the Problem and Plan You need to have a clear understanding of the problem to be solved. You then need to formulate some questions that will provide the necessary information to solve the problem. As the process develops, and information is gathered, further lines of enquiry may arise.	• Discuss what better concentration means and how it would be evident in a classroom. • Consider making some observations in lessons. • Which lessons would you observe? • Does the age of pupils make a difference? • Does the ability set make a difference?
Decide what Data to Collect You need to decide what data you will collect, how it will be collected and how much you will collect (sample size). Think about different types of data such as qualitative and quantitive, discrete and continuous.	• One possibility is to select some pupils in a class and observe them. • The lesson could be divided up into intervals in which these pupils are concentrating or not. • At the end of the lesson each pupil would have a total time. • Consider the use of secondary data.
Collect Data from a Variety of Sources Consider observations, experiments, surveys, and primary and secondary sources. Use suitable data collection techniques, such as the various sampling methods, and give thought to how you will record the data so that it will be easy to work with later.	• A suitable data sheet would be needed to use in the classroom observations. • It may be possible to research the subject on the Internet.
Process and Represent the Data Use relevant statistical measures that summarise the data and consider graphs and charts to represent it.	• You could calculate the mean concentration time for boys and for girls. • The data might be represented using box plots for example.
Interpret and Discuss the Data Consider the data in terms of the original problem and the questions asked. Decide whether the problem has been answered or if further lines of enquiry now need to be followed in a new cycle.	• Use the statistics calculated along with the charts to make comparisons and draw conclusions.
Possible follow-up enquiry	• Do girls / boys do better in single sex lessons / schools?

Collecting Data

Some Definitions

Primary Data: data which has been directly obtained first hand, either by yourself or by someone under your direction. It can be collected by questionnaire, survey, observation, experiment or data logging.

Secondary Data: data which has been obtained independently by an external agency and which may be already stored either in printed or electronic form, e.g. published statistics, data from the Internet.

The Population: all of the items you are investigating.

The Sample: the limited number of items that you have selected to represent the whole population.

A Random Sample: a sample in which every item of the population has an equal chance of being selected. In practice this means taking great care to spread the 'randomness' over as large an area as possible and to take repeated surveys and work out averages.

Reasons for Sampling

Information is a hugely powerful tool in modern society but clearly it is impossible to survey huge populations. Sampling allows us to look at a cross-section of the population, making the process much quicker and much cheaper! Samples are used widely to:

- Inform opinion polls.
- Market research.
- To produce T.V. viewing figures.
- To provide trend analysis.

Identifying Bias in Samples

Consider the following bad examples of sampling:
- A recent survey suggests that 82% of the population prefer Rugby League to Football. The survey was conducted in St Helens.
- A High Street survey reveals that 76% of men aged between 18 and 42 go to the pub at least once a week. The survey was conducted at 11pm.
- A telephone survey suggests that 100% of the population has at least one telephone in their house.

In order to be unbiased, every individual in the population must have an equal chance of being included in the sample. This means taking into account...
– the time of day of the survey
– the age range
– relative affluence
– the geographical area
– ethnicity
– lifestyle

However, you must also remember that the bigger the sample size, the more representative it is likely to be (assuming of course that you have minimised all the other potential areas of bias).

Collecting Data

Collecting Data by Observation

Collecting data by observation can be laborious and time consuming but for some things it is the best way. For instance, a traffic survey might be done in this way to reveal the volume of traffic using a bridge. You must remember to ask yourself whether the survey is being conducted at and for an appropriate time.

Collecting Data by Experiment

People involved in the Sciences use experiments to gather data to support their hypotheses. The key things to remember are that…

- the experiment must be repeated an appropriate number of times
- the experiment must be capable of being repeated by someone else.

Collecting Data by Questionnaire

Questionnaires are skillfully designed forms that are used to conduct surveys of a sample of the population.

Designing a Questionnaire

Good questionnaires have the following things in common:

- They are not too long, i.e. never more than 10 questions, but less if possible.
- They contain questions which are easily understood and do not cause confusion.
- They ask for simple, short answers, e.g. Yes/No, Like/Don't Like or Male/Female
- They avoid vague words like Tall, Old, Fast, Good, etc.
- The questions do not show any bias, e.g. 'Do you prefer watching rugby or hockey?' rather than 'Do you agree that rugby is a more watchable game than hockey?'
- They only contain relevant questions.

Example

Yasmin decides to test the hypothesis that 'Parents would prefer the school holidays to be shorter' by using the following questionnaire.

This tests whether the questionnaire is relevant to this person

The answer may be affected by the size of the family!

The answer may turn out to be dependent upon the age of the person's children!

This tells us whether or not the person will see a lot of his/her children over the holidays!

This avoids asking a 'loaded question', i.e. it avoids bias

QUESTIONNAIRE

1. Do you have children of school age?
   Yes ❑ No ❑

2. How many children do you have?
   1 ❑ 2 ❑ 3 ❑ 4+ ❑

3. To which age group do they belong?
   11-13 ❑ 14-16 ❑ 17-18 ❑

4. Are you in full time employment?
   Yes ❑ No ❑

5. Do you think the school holidays are…
   Too Short? ❑
   Too Long? ❑
   Just Right? ❑

From the answers, Yasmin could do the following:

1. Reject any responses from people who aren't parents.
2. Analyse the data to see if family size, age range and employment status affect the answers.
3. Come up with a pretty good answer to her original hypothesis.

Sorting Data

Discrete and Continuous Data

Data comes in many different forms. To make sense of the data it is often sorted and collated. There are two different types of numerical data that you can record for sorting and collating.

Discrete data is data that can only have certain values. For example, the number of goals a football team can score in a match is 0, 1, 2, 3, 4, etc. They cannot have a score in between, like 0.5, 1.6, 2.2, etc.

Continuous data is data that can have any value. It tends to be obtained by reading measuring instruments. The accuracy of the data is dependent on the precision of the equipment.

Tally Charts and Frequency Tables

Very often the best way to sort and collate discrete or continuous data is to draw a tally chart and a frequency table.

Example

Below are the results of the games involving Germany, in Round 1 through to the semi-finals of an International Hockey Tournament.

Germany 4 Costa Rica 2	Germany 2 Sweden 0
Germany 1 Poland 0	Germany 4 Argentina 2
Germany 0 Brazil 3	Germany 0 Italy 2

Sort the number of goals scored per game by each team by drawing a tally chart and a frequency table.

Since the range of data here is narrow (e.g. from 0 to 4 goals scored) each value can be included individually in the tally chart and frequency table. As you complete the tally column always tick off each number as you go along. This makes sure that you don't include the same number twice or miss any out.

The numbers in the frequency column are simply the number of tallies. Remember to add them up, as this total is equal to the total number of pieces of data (not, in this example, the total number of goals scored!).

The data in this example is discrete, however, the same process would apply for continuous data.

Germany 4̸ Costa Rica 2̸	Germany 2̸ Sweden 0̸
Germany 1̸ Poland 0̸	Germany 4̸ Argentina 2̸
Germany 0̸ Brazil 3̸	Germany 0̸ Italy 2̸

Number of goals scored	Tally	Frequency of that no. of goals being scored by a team
0	IIII	4
1	I	1
2	IIII	4
3	I	1
4	II	2
		Total = 12

Sorting Data

Using Class Intervals

Sometimes, unlike the example on the previous page, the data is so widespread that it is impractical to include each value in the tally chart and frequency table individually. When this happens, the data is sorted into groups called class intervals, where each class interval represents a range of values.

Example

Temperatures home and abroad

Amsterdam	19	Cairo	34	Majorca	27	New York	32
Athens	33	Cardiff	16	Manchester	12	Newcastle	13
Barbados	29	Dublin	15	Miami	26	Paris	20
Barcelona	26	Jersey	20	Milan	28	Peking	33
Berlin	23	London	21	Montreal	22	Prague	26
Bermuda	28	Madrid	33	Moscow	15	Rhodes	28

As you can see, the data here is widespread, e.g. from 12°C to 34°C. Out of practicality, the temperature values are arranged in groups of five in our tally chart and frequency table.

The class interval $10 \leqslant T < 15$ would include any temperature reading equal to or greater than 10°C and less than 15°C (a temperature reading of 15°C is included in the next class interval) and so on.

Remember to total the numbers in the frequency column to make sure they add up to the total number of locations (pieces of data).

The data in this example is continuous, however, the same process would apply for discrete data.

Recorded Temperatures, $T(°C)$	Tally	Frequency of Temperatures Falling Within that Range
$10 \leqslant T < 15$	II	2
$15 \leqslant T < 20$	IIII	4
$20 \leqslant T < 25$	⊦⊦⊦⊦	5
$25 \leqslant T < 30$	⊦⊦⊦⊦ III	8
$30 \leqslant T < 35$	⊦⊦⊦⊦	5
		Total = 24

Two Important Points:
- The format of class intervals can vary. The following class intervals could have been used to give the same results for the data above: 10–14, 15–19, 20–24, etc.
- The range of each class interval depends on the total range of the data. If the total range of the data is large and the range of each class interval is small, then your frequency table would have a lot of rows. Aim to have no more than 10 lines in your table!

Sorting Data

Stem and Leaf Diagrams

A stem and leaf diagram sorts data into groups. An advantage over frequency tables is that they enable you to get more of a feel for the 'shape' of distribution. For example, the following data shows the length of time (in minutes) it took 30 pupils to complete a test, arranged in ascending order:

8, 8, 9, 15, 15, 16, 16, 17, 18, 18, 20, 21, 21, 22, 23, 26, 27, 27, 28, 28, 29, 33, 34, 34, 35, 39, 39, 42, 48, 49

This data can be represented using a stem and leaf diagram by taking the tens to form the 'stem' of the diagram and the units to form the 'leaves'.

The end product is similar to a frequency table. However, besides allowing you to visualise the 'shape' of the data, it can be used to identify the modal class, i.e. the 20–29 group and the median (24.5 – between the 15th and 16th piece of data as there are 30 values.)

Stem	Leaves										
0	8	8	9								
1	5	5	6	6	7	8	8				
2	0	1	1	2	3	6	7	7	8	8	9
3	3	4	4	5	9	9					
4	2	8	9								

Key: **1** **5** means **15**

Two-way Tables

Two-way tables simply show two sets of information, one vertically and the other horizontally. Information organised in this way can actually result in you gaining more information than you started with.

Example

'In a survey, 200 Year 7 and 8 pupils were asked if they preferred Maths or Science. 73 out of 110 Year 7 pupils preferred Maths, and in total 82 pupils preferred Science.' This could lead to the table below…

	Year 7	Year 8	Total
Science			82
Maths	73		
Total	110		200

… that can be used to work out the missing data.

	Year 7	Year 8	Total
Science	37	45	82
Maths	73	45	118
Total	110	90	200

Notice that in the original table there was no data for Year 8 … now it's all there!

Various Types of Table

Tables can be arranged in many different ways to suit the purpose for which they are intended. Remember, the idea is to make the information as accessible as possible, so you've got to give a bit of thought as to how you want to present it.

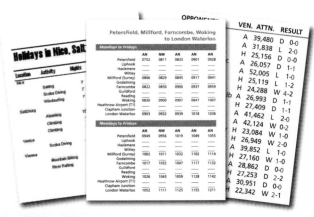

Displaying Data

Displaying Data from a Table

The best way of displaying data that has been sorted into a frequency table is to draw a graph.

Here is the frequency table for the number of goals scored in games involving Germany in Round 1 through to the semi-finals of an International Hockey Tournament (we only include the tally column when we are sorting the data).

No. of goals scored	Frequency
0	4
1	1
2	4
3	1
4	2

The data above can be displayed in various ways:

Dual and Composite Bar Charts

Data from two or more groups may be shown on a single chart. A **dual** bar chart shows the bars side by side and a **composite** bar chart combines the responses in a single bar. A key is needed to explain what each part of the chart represents.

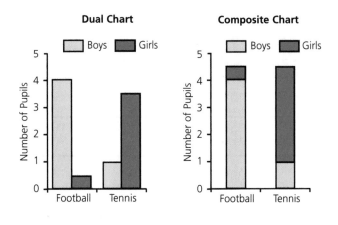

A Pictogram

Simple diagrams are used to display data. Since our data is about hockey we have used a ball. Don't forget to use the key when reading the pictogram.

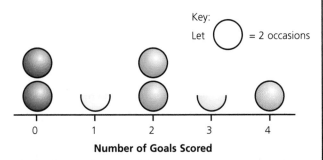

A Bar Graph

Bars or columns are used to display data. Make sure that the height of each bar is equal to the correct frequency.

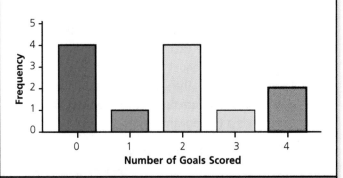

A Vertical Line Graph

This graph is very similar to the bar graph except that lines are drawn instead of bars. Make sure that the height of each line is equal to the correct frequency.

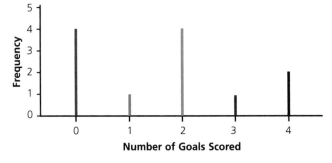

A Line Graph

This is not always the most suitable way to display discrete data, as the lines joining the points have no meaning!

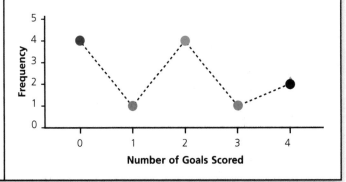

Displaying Data

Displaying Grouped Data

Data that has been grouped together and sorted, using class intervals, in a frequency table can also be displayed by drawing a graph.

Here is the frequency table for the recorded temperatures for various locations at home and abroad.

Recorded Temperatures T(°C)	Frequency
10 ⩽ T < 15	2
15 ⩽ T < 20	4
20 ⩽ T < 25	5
25 ⩽ T < 30	8
30 ⩽ T < 35	5

The data above can be displayed in various ways:

A Frequency Diagram

A frequency diagram is much like a bar chart but there are no gaps between the bars and the horizontal axis has a continuous scale. In the example below the values 10, 15, 20… are spaced equally, as opposed to writing 10-15, 15-20, and so on. The intervals always have equal width on a frequency diagram. Another word for this type of diagram is a **histogram**.

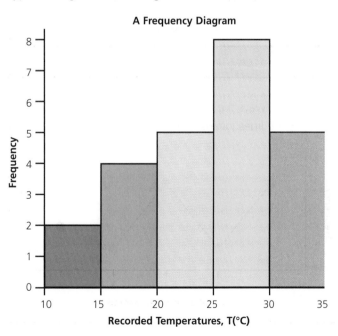

A Frequency Polygon

With a frequency polygons you need to mark the middle of the top of each bar in the frequency diagram with a cross and then join up these crosses with straight lines.

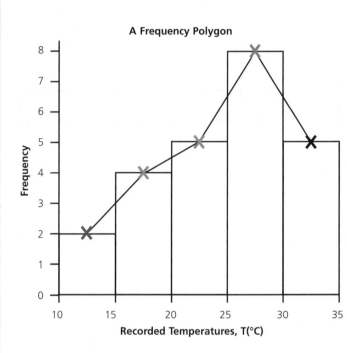

You may be asked to draw a frequency polygon directly from the frequency table. You must remember to plot the crosses at the correct frequency exactly over the middle of the class intervals, e.g. for **10 ⩽ T < 15**, plot the cross above 12.5

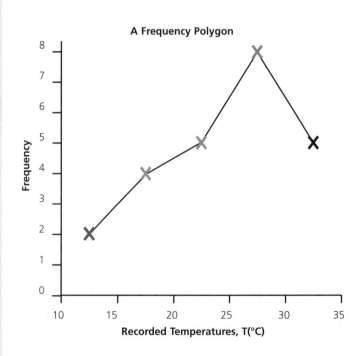

Displaying Data

Scatter Diagrams

A scatter diagram is a graph that has two sets of data plotted on it at the same time. When plotted, the points may show a certain trend or correlation. A correlation is defined as the 'strength of relationship between two variables'.

Positive Correlation
As one increases, the other also increases, e.g. the number of ice creams sold and daytime temperature.

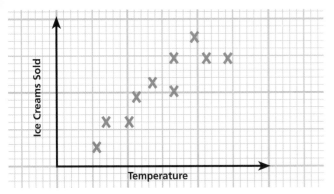

Negative Correlation
As one increases, the other decreases or vice versa, e.g. amount of petrol left in tank and distance travelled by car.

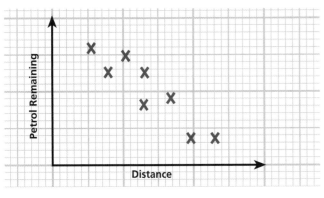

Zero Correlation
No obvious trend between the two, e.g. length of hair and height. Remember that zero correlation does not necessarily imply 'no relationship' but merely 'no linear relationship'.

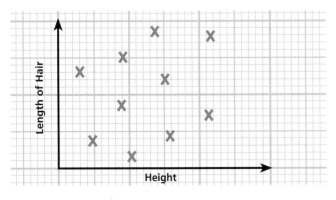

Line of Best Fit

A line of best fit is a straight line that passes through the points so that we have as many points above the line as we have below the line. A line of best fit can only be drawn if our points show positive or negative correlation. Below are four different examples of lines of best fit.

A and **B** are **poor** lines of best fit. They both have the same number of points above and below the line but these points are bunched together and not spread out.

C and **D** are **good** lines of best fit. They both have the same number of points above and below the lines and these points are spread out.

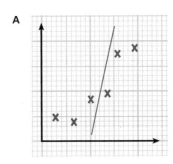

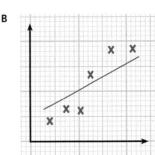

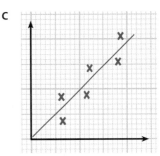

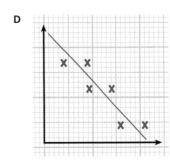

Displaying Data

Using a Line of Best Fit

Example

The table gives the maths mark and science mark for 12 pupils in their end of year examinations.

Maths Mark	Science Mark
60	56
30	30
46	47
89	98
48	61
78	77
26	38
38	51
91	89
20	25
65	80
73	87

a) Draw a scatter diagram, including a line of best fit, to show the marks.

b) Tim was absent from his science exam but he achieved a mark of 65 in his maths exam. Use your graph to work out an estimated science mark for Tim.

c) Jenny achieved a mark of 42 in her science exam but she was absent for her maths exam. Again use your graph to work out an estimated maths mark for Jenny.

a)

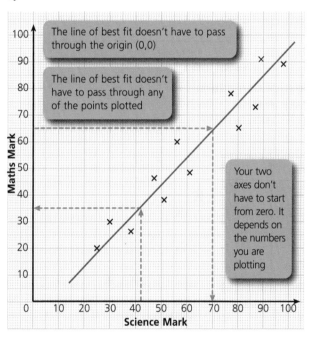

The line of best fit doesn't have to pass through the origin (0,0)

The line of best fit doesn't have to pass through any of the points plotted

Your two axes don't have to start from zero. It depends on the numbers you are plotting

b) Go to 65 on the maths axis and then draw a dotted line across to (→) the line of best fit and then down to (↓) the science axis. This is Tim's estimated science mark.

Answer is 70

c) Go to 42 on the science axis and then draw a dotted line up to (↑) the line of best fit and then across to (←) the maths axis. This is Jenny's estimated maths mark.

Answer is 35

Displaying Data

Drawing Pie Charts

Another way of displaying sorted data is to draw a pie chart. A pie chart is a circle which is split into different sectors. Here are the results of a survey carried out among 18 pupils to find their favourite sport.

Favourite Sport	Frequency (no. of Pupils)
Football	7
Tennis	3
Hockey	8
	Total = 18

Before we can draw our pie chart we need to calculate the **angle** of the sector representing each sport. To do this we work out the fraction of the pupils for each sport, then multiply this fraction by 360°.

Favourite Sport	Frequency of Pupils	Angle to be Shown
Football	Total number of pupils → $\frac{7}{18}$ ← Number who liked football	$\frac{7}{18} \times 360° = \mathbf{140°}$
Tennis	Total number of pupils → $\frac{3}{18}$ ← Number who liked tennis	$\frac{3}{18} \times 360° = \mathbf{60°}$
Hockey	Total number of pupils → $\frac{8}{18}$ ← Number who liked hockey	$\frac{8}{18} \times 360° = \mathbf{160°}$
		Total = 360°

We can now draw our pie chart. Always measure all angles carefully with a protractor and make sure that you always use the scale on your protractor that starts at 0°.

1 Pick a starting point and draw a radius:

2 Measure and mark 140° for football:

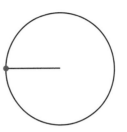

3 Measure and mark 60° for tennis:

4 Check the remainder (for hockey) is 160°:

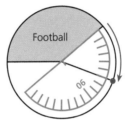
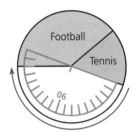

5 The completed pie chart will now look like this:

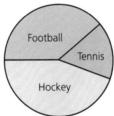

Getting Information from Pie Charts

Getting information from a pie chart is very similar to drawing a pie chart except you need to work backwards. If the pie chart above shows the favourite sport for 18 pupils, the first thing we need to do is measure all the angles. We can then work out the number of pupils for each sport.

Favourite Sport	Proportion of Pupils	Number of Pupils
Football	Total no. of ° for a circle → $\frac{140°}{360°}$ ← Number of ° for football	$\frac{140°}{360°} \times 18 = \mathbf{7}$
Tennis	Total no. of ° for a circle → $\frac{60°}{360°}$ ← Number of ° for tennis	$\frac{60°}{360°} \times 18 = \mathbf{3}$
Hockey	Total no. of ° for a circle → $\frac{160°}{360°}$ ← Number of ° for hockey	$\frac{160°}{360°} \times 18 = \mathbf{8}$
		Total = 18 pupils

Averages & Spread

Describing Data

An average is a representative value. There are three methods of finding the average: the mean, the median and the mode. Depending on the data, one method may be better suited to giving a good representative value than another. However, an average does not give any sense of the spread of the data as may be illustrated by the following example.

10, 10, 10	mean = 10
9, 10, 11	mean = 10
8, 10, 12	mean = 10
7, 10, 13	mean = 10

The example shows that the mean is totally insensitive to the changes in the spread of the data.

To measure the spread of the data we need a different measure, such as the range.

Examples

Sam has the following coins in his pocket. What he has is a distribution of numbers (the different valued coins).

① Mean

The mean is given by:

$$\text{Mean} = \frac{\textbf{Sum of all the values}}{\textbf{Number of values}}$$

$$= \frac{1p+5p+1p+20p+10p+5p+1p+1p+10p}{9 \text{ (number of coins)}}$$

$$= \frac{54p}{9} = \textbf{6p}$$

② Median

The median is the middle value, providing that all the numbers have been arranged in order, lowest to highest.

1p, 1p, 1p, 1p, 5p, 5p, 10p, 10p, 20p

1̶p̶, 1̶p̶, 1̶p̶, 1̶p̶, 5p, 5̶p̶, 1̶0̶p̶, 10̶p̶, 2̶0̶p̶

> Arrange in order

Median = 5p

> Tick off from the two ends to find the middle value

If you tick off from the two ends and are left with two numbers in the middle, then the median is the number halfway between those two numbers

(e.g. for 1̶, 1̶, 1, 2, 2̶, 2̶ **Median = 1.5**)

③ Mode

The mode is the most **common value**, i.e. the number that occurs most frequently.

Mode = 1p

> 1p coin occurs more times than any other coin

④ Range

The range is the **difference** between the **highest** and the **lowest** value.

Range = 20p − 1p = **19p**

Averages & Spread

Mean, Median, Mode and Range from a Frequency Table

Here is the frequency table for the number of goals scored in games involving Germany, from Round 1 through to the semi-finals of an International Hockey Tournament.

The data in this frequency table is discrete.

Number of Goals Scored by the Teams (x)	Frequency (f)	Frequency × No. of Goals Scored (fx)	
0	4	4 × 0 = **0**	4 teams have scored 0 goals. Total number of goals scored = 4 × 0 = 0
1	1	1 × 1 = **1**	1 team has scored 1 goal. Total number of goals scored = 1 × 1 = 1
2	4	4 × 2 = **8**	4 teams have scored 2 goals. Total number of goals scored = 4 × 2 = 8
3	1	1 × 3 = **3**	1 team have scored 3 goals. Total number of goals scored = 1 × 3 = 3
4	2	2 × 4 = **8**	2 teams have scored 4 goals. Total number of goals scored = 2 × 4 = 8
	Total = 12	Total = 20	Total number of goals scored = 0 + 1 + 8 + 3 + 8 = 20

Mean

To calculate the mean another column is added (in green) to our frequency table to calculate the total number of goals scored.

$$\text{Mean} = \frac{\text{Total number of goals scored } (fx)}{\text{Total frequency}}$$

$$= \frac{20}{12} = 1.\dot{6} \text{ goals per team}$$

Mode

Mode = 0 and 2 goals

(these occur more times than any of the others).

Note: You may well be asked to identify the modal class from a frequency table involving grouped data. In the stated example on p108 the modal class is $25 \leqslant T < 30$ since this class interval has the highest frequency (i.e. it occurs the most number of times).

Median

Since we have 12 pieces of data, the median number of goals is halfway between the 6th and 7th piece of data (with an even number you always end up with two numbers in the middle).

4 Teams Scored	1 Team Scored	4 Teams Scored	1 Team Scored	2 Teams Scored
0̸ 0̸ 0̸ 0̸	1̸	②② 2̸ 2̸	3̸	4̸ 4̸

$$\text{Median} = \frac{2 + 2}{2} = \textbf{2 goals}$$

Range

Range = 4 goals – 0 goals

= **4 goals**

Averages & Spread

Mean, Median, Mode and Range from a Frequency Table of Grouped Data

Here is the frequency table for the recorded temperatures for various locations at home and abroad.

The data in this frequency table is continuous.

Recorded Temp., T (°C)	Frequency (f)	Mid-Temp. Values (x)	Frequency × Mid-Temp. Values (fx)
10 ≤ T < 15	2	12.5	2 × 12.5 = **25**
15 ≤ T < 20	4	17.5	4 × 17.5 = **70**
20 ≤ T < 25	5	22.5	5 × 22.5 = **112.5**
25 ≤ T < 30	8	27.5	8 × 27.5 = **220**
30 ≤ T < 35	5	32.5	5 × 32.5 = **162.5**
	Total = 24		**Total = 590**

These are class intervals

These are halfway values for our class intervals

Estimated Mean

With grouped data, the individual values are unknown. Therefore we have to use 'mid-interval value' to provide an **estimate** of the mean. To calculate the mean this time we need to add two further columns (in green) to our frequency table.

$$\text{Mean} = \frac{\text{Total of Recorded Temperatures } (fx)}{\text{Total frequency}}$$

$$= \frac{590}{24}$$

$$= \textbf{24.58°C}$$

Mode

Again we don't get an exact mode but we are able to determine which class interval or group is the **modal class**. Modal Class is **25 ≤ T < 30** since this class interval has the highest frequency (i.e. it occurs the most number of times).

Median

With continuous data we don't get an exact value for the median, but we are able to determine which class interval or group it is in. The table opposite has 24 pieces of data and so the median is halfway between the 12th and 13th piece of data. Using the frequency column, the median is in the **25 ≤ T < 30** class interval.

Formulae Sheet

These are the formulae issued by Edexcel for foundation tier students.

Area of a trapezium $= \frac{1}{2}(a + b)h$

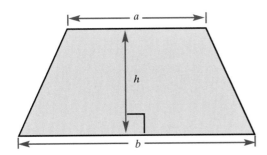

Volume of a prism = area of cross section x length

Notes

Index

3-D shapes
   Drawing solids using isometric paper 81
   Solids 81

A
Accuracy, checking your answers for 29
Addition and subtraction of whole numbers 10
Algebraic expressions 30
   Collecting like terms 30
Angles
   Acute, right, obtuse and reflex 52
   Alternate 53
   Corresponding 53
   On a straight line 52
   Parallel lines 53
Area 66
   Common shapes 66
   Estimation 66
   Formula for area of parallelogram 67
   Formula for area of a triangle 67

B
BIDMAS 15

C
Circles 68
   Area 70
   Circumference 69
Collecting data
   By experiment 97
   By observation 97
   By questionnaire 97
   Definitions 96
   Designing a questionnaire 97
   Identifying bias in samples 96
   Sampling, reasons for 96
Compound measures
   Fuel efficiency 89
   Speed 89
Congruent shapes 61
Constructions
   Angle of 60° and 90° 77
   Bisector of an angle 78
   Midpoint and perpendicular bisector of a line segment 78
   Perpendicular from a point on a line 78
   Perpendicular from a point to a line 78
   Regular hexagon inside a circle 79
   Triangles 77
Cube roots of positive numbers 14

D
Decimals
   Addition and subtraction 6
   Division by powers of 10 7
   Division by whole and decimal numbers 7
   Multiplication by powers of 10. 6
   Multiplication by whole and and decimal numbers 6
   Ordering 5
   Recurring and terminating 5
Decimal numbers
   Place value 5
   Money 5
Decimal places
   Rounding a number 4
Describing data 106
Division of positive numbers by decimal numbers between 0 and 1. 7
Drawing to size and scale 85

E
Enlargement
   Perimeter and area 86
   Volume 86
Estimated mean 108
Estimating answers 29
Everyday maths
   Household bills 26
   Purchasing on credit 25
   Simple interest 25
   Understanding tables and charts 26
   VAT 25

F
Factorisation 33
Formulae
   Changing the subject 36
   Deriving formulae 37
   Using formulae 37
Formulae sheet 109

Fractions 24
   Addition 18
   Cancelling fractions 16
   Equivalent fractions 16
   Fraction of a quantity 19
   Improper fractions and mixed numbers 17
   Multiplication and division 18
   One quantity as a fraction of another 19
   Ordering 17
   Simple fractions 16
   Subtraction 18
Fractions, Decimals and Percentages 23, 24

G
Graphs
   Conversion 50
   Distance time (travel) 51
   Finding the equation of a straight line 45
   Of linear functions 42-43
   Quadratic functions 47
   Real-life situations 49, 50
   Solving equations 48
   $x = a$ number 44
   $y = a$ number 44
   $y = x$ and $x = y$ 44

I
Integers 11
   Addition and subtraction 12
   Multiplication and division 12
   Ordering integers 11
Irregular polygons 57
   Interior and exterior angles 57

L
Linear equations
   Problem solving 35
   With the unknown on both sides of the equation 35
   With the unknown on one side 34
Linear inequalities
   Four kinds of inequality 46
Locus 80
Long multiplication and long division of whole numbers 10

M
Map scales 85
Mean, median, mode and range from a frequency table 107
Mean, median, mode and range from a frequency table of grouped data 108
Measurements
   Angles 90
   Converting between metric and imperial units 87
   Converting one metric unit and another 87
   Lines 90
   Metric and imperial units 87
Multiplication and division of whole numbers by powers of 10. 10
Multiplying out brackets 33

N
Nets for solids 82
Number Properties
   Cube numbers 13
   Factors (divisors) 8
   Highest common factor 9
   Lowest (least) common multiple 9
   Multiples 8
   Prime numbers 8
   Prime factor form 9
   Reciprocals 8
   Square numbers 13

P
Percentages
   Calculating a percentage of a quantity 20
   Expressing one quantity as a percentage of another quantity 20
   Income tax 22
   Increasing by a percentage 21
   Mental methods 21
   Multipliers 22
   Reducing by a percentage 21
   Simple percentages 20
   VAT 22
Perimeter 65
Plans and elevations 82
Plotting points 41

Index

Polygons
    Irregular 57
    Regular 58
Powers of 10. 13
Powers of negative numbers 13
Probability
    Equally likely outcomes 92
    Importance of sample
        size 94
    Language of 92
    Nature of 91
    Outcomes of single
        events 93
    Outcomes of two successive
        events 93
    Probability scale and the
        language of 91
    Relative frequency 94
    Theoretical 94
Problem solving in statistics 95
Pythagoras 63
    Calculate the length of one
        of the shorter sides 64

Q
Quadrilaterals
    Interior angles 56
    Types 56

R
Ratio and proportion 27
    Dividing a quantity 28
    Fractions 27
    Increasing and decreasing 28
Regular polygons 58
Rounding numbers 4
Rules of indices 14
    For algebra 31

S
Sequences
    Finding the nth term of an
        arithmetic sequence 40
    nth term of a sequence 40
    Number patterns and
        sequences 39
Significant figures
    Rounding a number 4
Similar shapes 62
Sorting data
    Correlations 103
    Discrete and continuous
        data 98
    Displaying data from a
        table 101
    Displaying grouped
        data 102

Drawing pie charts 105
Frequency diagram 102
Frequency polygon 102
Getting information from
    pie charts 105
Histogram 102
Line of best fit 103
Scatter diagrams 103
Stem and leaf
    diagrams 100
Tally charts and frequency
    tables 98
Two-way tables 100
Types of table 100
Using a line of best fit 104
Using class intervals 99
Square roots 14
Substitution 32
Surface area of solids 70
Symmetry
    Line or reflective 59
    Rotational 60

T
Tessellation 61
Three-figure bearings 88
Transformations
    Characteristics 76

Combination 76
Enlargement 75
Reflection 71-72
Rotation 73
Translation 74
Types 71
Trial and Improvement 38
Triangles
    Angles 54
    Types
        Equilateral 55
        Isosceles 55
        Right-angled 55
        Scalene 55

U
Understanding powers 13
Use of brackets 15

V
Volume 83
    Calculation of the volume
        of a solid made up of
        cubes 83
    Cuboid, of 83
    Cylinder, of 84
    Prism, of 83-84